WHEN THIS THING HAPPENED

Michael McKernan is a professional writer, reviewer, and commentator in the area of Australian history. He has written about war and society, the region, sport, and Australian politics. He was a senior lecturer in Australian history at the University of New South Wales before accepting the position of deputy director at the Australian War Memorial. Now working as a consultant historian, he is the author or editor of more than 20 books, including *The Strength of a Nation*, *Here is Their Spirit*, and *This War Never Ends*. He and his wife live in Canberra.

WHEN THIS THING HAPPENED

THE STORY OF A FATHER, A SON, AND THE WARS THAT CHANGED THEM

MICHAEL McKERNAN

SCRIBE
Melbourne • London

Scribe Publications
18–20 Edward St, Brunswick, Victoria, Australia 3056
2 John St, Clerkenwell, London, WC1N 2ES, United Kingdom

First published by Scribe 2015

Typeset in Adobe Caslon 11.5/16.5 pt by the publishers

Printed and bound in Australia by Griffin Press

The paper this book is printed on is certified against the Forest Stewardship Council® Standards. Griffin Press holds FSC chain of custody certification SGS-COC-005088. FSC promotes environmentally responsible, socially beneficial and economically viable management of the world's forests.

National Library of Australia Cataloguing-in-Publication data

McKernan, Michael, 1945- author.

When This Thing Happened / Michael McKernan.

9781925106893 (paperback)
9781925307160 (e-book)

1. War and families–Ukrainian. 2. War and families–Australia. 3. Ukrainians–Australia–Biography. 4. World War, 1914-1918–Personal narratives. 5. World War, 1939-1945–Personal narratives. 6. Vietnam War, 1961-1975–Personal narratives.

920.009291791

scribepublications.com.au
scribepublications.co.uk

This book is dedicated to Michael Stawyskyj's granddaughters,
Zoe, Natalia, Holly, and Lilli

Contents

ix
Prologue

1
Part One: Michael's Story

101
Part Two: Joe's Story

225
Epilogue

229
Acknowledgements

Prologue

The Wedding

The photograph, nicely framed, has been sitting on the dresser in our bedroom since we were married. It's a wedding photo, but not ours. It is a picture of Michael Stawyskyj and his bride, Anna, on their wedding day, presumably after the ceremony. They stand on a long stone stairway; she stands a step above him and therefore comes to just about his height. Anna drapes one arm affectionately over Michael's shoulder. Both hold half smiles for the camera, but their eyes tell us that they are very happy, as they should be on their wedding day.

The couple are nicely dressed, but in 'Sunday best', not the traditional costume of bride and groom. Anna wears a dark suit, with a skirt rather than pants, and a white blouse done up to the neck. She carries dark gloves in her right hand. She has neat shoes and stockings. Michael is in a light jacket, seemingly woollen, with a vest, possibly knitted; he has a white shirt and a striped tie. His slacks are white, and he wears dark shoes. He, too, carries gloves, in his left hand. Both Michael and Anna have large white bows, made of ribbon, beneath a small spray of flowers on their lapels, signifying that this is their wedding day. They seem assured and confident as they gaze at the camera. The future seems to be on their side.

The past and the present, as you will discover, are something else. Both had been taken from their Ukrainian villages when relatively young: Michael at 17 or 18 years of age, his new wife at 15 years of age. They had worked for the Germans throughout the war, as a farm labourer and household skivvy, respectively. They were not free to come and go as they chose; they were not free to change jobs as better opportunities presented. They were to do the work they were directed to do by the authorities and those for whom they worked. They were moved to other places of employment by the authorities whenever the labour officer determined. They were not paid. They were, in effect, slaves. Wartime slaves in the cause of the Fatherland. Not their fatherland — Hitler's.

After the war, they were displaced persons. Part of a European army of millions, thrown into chaos by war, by bombing, through the loss of homes and lands, through the loss of jobs, through the loss of citizenship if their country was taken from them by post-war big-power decisions. Ukraine was no longer an independent entity, but had been swallowed up by Stalin's monster, the Union of Soviet Socialist Republics. It was certainly no place for those who had worked for the Germans, because those who had worked for the Germans were viewed — by Stalin and by all those who took their orders and their ideas from him, insanely — as collaborators. Perhaps, if ever they were to return home, they might be retrained in correct thought in a Siberian labour camp, but perhaps they might fall victim to a worse fate. The displaced-persons camps were awful, crowded, confused, and oppressive. Yet there was some hope in fleeing from home and Stalin.

But these are not good thoughts for a wedding day. It would have been a day of joy, of hopes for the future, of young people at the threshold of life. The bridal register, or whatever formality was involved, will tell you that she was Anna Gratz before she married. She had worked for the Germans throughout the war, and was placed in a Polish camp as a displaced person after the war. But she had heard of the Ukrainian camp nearby, which, as a Ukrainian, she would visit. Michael later told me, 'there was always people come together in the camp and talk, and get to know each other … she came to the Ukrainian camp to talk with Ukrainian people. We met there and decide to marry.'

It can't have been as simple and straightforward as that, or as lacking in romance. There must have been a courtship. There must have been long discussions of hopes for the future and aspirations for a life after war. The unending awful camp life could drain hope quickly and fatally. Michael was now 25 years of age; Anna was 21.

On this wedding day, they were joined by about six people, Michael said, but there was no party — who could afford that? There were no family members among the six wedding guests. Michael's parents and his brothers and sisters had been lost to him from the day the Germans drove him out of the village that had always been his home and took him to work, with millions of others, as their slave. What he would give to have his mother by his side on this day above all others! To introduce, shyly, Anna to his mother, and hope that his mother would approve. A good Ukrainian girl with fine values, high hopes, and a decent background. A Catholic girl — not Orthodox — to add the icing to the cake. What Anna would have given to have her own mother at the wedding, to fuss over her, to make sure that all was exactly as it should be on her day, and for her new husband. But it could not be; they could not go back. There was too much danger in a return home.

The wedding photo that we have is on the day of the civilian ceremony performed 'by the Germans', probably by a town official. It is after this ceremony that we see them photographed. How much of what they are wearing is borrowed from the friends who have gathered to wish them well? Yet it all seems to fit nicely. How could a young displaced person find and afford stockings? Well, Anna had. Is this a proper wedding, this civil ceremony, they asked themselves, so familiar with the village weddings at home of family and friends. Of the priest and the long service, and everyone taking part, singing and praying the ancient liturgy, a part of Ukrainian tradition for nearly a thousand years.

There had been an earlier church wedding in the camp, from which we still have the documentation to show that they were validly married in the eyes of the Church. It was nothing too grand. 'We have a church marriage, too, but there was not ceremony, nothing. I just go with her to the priest and get married.' That was important because Michael and Anna were both religious people. Pleasingly and importantly for them, they were both Catholic, when Orthodox Christianity, either Russian or Greek, heavily predominated in their former country. There were few Ukrainian Catholic Christians, in communion with the Pope in Rome, but both Michael and Anna were among that small minority. There had been a priest in the camp who could marry them, probably a Ukrainian priest, perhaps in much the same difficulty as they were themselves. Homeless and battling for his future.

There would have been music later on, too, because Michael loved singing and had a fine voice, and he'd been part of an informal choir all through his years in Germany, whenever the 'Ukrainian boys and girls' were allowed a few hours off. So there wasn't a party, or a formal church ceremony, as Michael thought of these things, but enough was done in the right way to mark this as a special day.

As a married couple, they were now allotted their own room in the camp. They were housed in former German army barracks, a three-storey building made of stone — 'nice rooms', Michael said — and now a room of their own. They would talk and talk of what they hoped for from life, of where they would go, of how they would make a family, in America, in Canada, where? Marriage gave stability and urgency to these dreams. To begin at once. A home of their own. Jobs where they could earn good money. Above all, security. An end to war and slavery, to orders and control; an end to fear and uncertainty. To live the kind of life their parents had lived: with children, good food, honest work, friends, and community. Was this too much to hope for? Out of this camp, soon, please God, and into a life that could then begin.

The wedding day gave promise of all that. It was a day of hope and optimism, of a future at last, when they might say what they wanted from life. When they might say that these years of slavery and uncertainty were behind them, that the families they so achingly missed would be recreated in the likenesses of their own parents' marriages. This was a day of goodwill and good cheer. It was a day when they stood in the doorway to their future together.

The Storytellers

My father, Fred McKernan, was a superb storyteller. His stock-in-trade was tales from his own earlier life, tales from his working day, wry observations of the world around him. His own father died in 1925 when Fred was 15. There was no money in the family, and Fred left school to start work at the Vacuum Oil Company as an office boy. Later, but soon enough, he was tasked with travelling around the state of Victoria, recording correct usage at the various Vacuum service stations. It was lonely work — he was too young even to join the other commercial travellers for drinks before and after dinner. Fred consulted a priest at his former school for advice about the loneliness. 'Read, Fred, read' was the answer, and my father began on a lifetime of reading. His storytelling, I think, emerged from his love of reading.

By the time I was aware of life around me, Fred had his own business as a public accountant. It was a good practice, so far as I could judge; it certainly fed and clothed us. I don't say that Fred never lost a client, but many of those for whom he kept the books had been clients for many years, and he polished and burnished their characters for us over the years. Whether he had a particularly strong collection of scallywags, trimmers, and miscreants, I couldn't say, but he seemed forever to be rescuing his people from their own worst instincts and keeping them just that little bit on-side with the tax authorities. Not every single one of his clients had imbibed too generously on the spirit of Wilkins Micawber, but enough had to keep us amused. Dinner at our place was a lively time of storytelling.

My father died, too young, at the age of 67 — and how I missed that voice and the elaborate, careful structure of his stories. Mr Bellanto, Mr Enever, Mr Grigson, their quirks, their mischief, their mistakes in the name of a quid, all disappeared overnight. I missed my father's wide-eyed amazement at 'what some people would get up to', his chuckle, and the clever construction of the story that he and we knew was probably nine-parts fabrication. Perhaps I tried to shape my own storytelling on my father's model, but here, truthfully, was a boy trying to take on a man's role.

When I first met Michalina, the woman who would become my wife, I recognised a certain reluctance in her to introduce me to her family. They were just ordinary folk, she warned me. 'Dad worked in a factory all his life,' she said, 'as did my mum, although she died a couple of years ago. My younger brother is just out of law school, still living at home, and may do alright, time will tell. And then there's Joe, and he's in a wheelchair without too much to say for himself. Dad built the house himself,' she continued, 'and it's just a Fairfield fibro, three bedrooms with a large back room added on for Joe and a nice porch out the back.'

It all sounded fine to me. To have raised Michalina, with her values and integrity (as I was beginning to discover), they must have been pretty good people, I figured. Anyway, be open to people, I counselled myself, and take as you find. It had served me well in the past, in the workplace, among my students, and in the veterans' community, with whom I had become increasingly involved. Imagine my surprise on first meeting Michael Stawyskyj, my future father-in-law, as, even then, I vaguely intuited him to be. A tough, nuggety little man, endearingly shy, made sinewy and undoubtedly strong from long years of heavy lifting.

On that first visit, I observed and, to a limited extent, participated in the ritual that was the pattern of all Michalina's regular returns to the family home in Bell Crescent. First, she would inspect the house to make sure that Dad was coping. Clean? Tick. Enough and the right food in the fridge? Tick. Then outside. Lawns mowed and edges neat? Tick. Then the vegie patch. The pride with which Michael showed new growth, bounty, maybe even new lines. Well-weeded? Tick. Soil nicely turned-over? Tick. Nothing overripe or left to rot on the ground? Tick. It wasn't that Michalina was her father's keeper, nothing like that at all. It was just that he liked to show that he was keeping up with things, working hard, running a tight ship. Everything always as it had been when his dear wife was in charge.

Honour satisfied, Michalina might get on with the dull domestic jobs to lighten his load a bit, put on some washing, peg out the clothes on the line, or go off to the Neeta centre in Fairfield for the shopping, relieving him of that onerous, boring, necessary chore, for the next week at least. Would you like a beer, he would say to me, and then we would sit in comfortable chairs on the back porch; Michalina, back from the shopping, would prepare the meal, and he would have a few hours just to himself. A little moment in the week when he was not responsible for everything, not responding to Joe's next call for coffee or a cigarette, not keeping an eye on the clock for when he should start cooking the next meal. A little time for himself. It was then that I discovered that I had found the second great storyteller in my life. First there was Fred McKernan, long since gone, and now Michael

Stawyskyj, shyly bringing forth the stories of a remarkable life.

Michael spoke with an accent. He had seven languages, he said, matter-of-factly, and 'English was my worst'. I found that he spoke correct English, with a complex and rich vocabulary. But an accent. Once, I criticised the incoming Howard government. 'No,' said Michael, 'I won't have it; at least he sticks up for the butlers.' Butlers, as a class, didn't seem to be doing it too tough, I imagined, not that I had ever given them much thought. Did people still have butlers, I wondered. But at least, in Michael's view, Howard was looking after them. Howard's butlers? Think, think. Oh, battlers. Howard's battlers. It was the accent.

So there we were, on the back porch, beer in hand, or coffee if it was that time of day. You didn't need to ask a question to start Michael off. 'Tell me about the time …' would intrude on the storyteller's art. Nor would he introduce a story as a logical segue from something else. 'That reminds me of the time when …' was not part of his repertoire. We might be talking of current politics, or sport (he had an intense dislike of Shane Warne, but he had adopted the Sydney Swans as his passion because it was mine), or local happenings. And then he would start — but what prompted him, I could never tell. Probably just the sheer joy of telling a story to a listener who seemed engaged.

'I was on a farm in Germany. There were other Ukrainian boys in the district, and we met up from time to time for songs or a yarn. But mostly I was by myself with the family. At meal times, they all sat together around a big table, but I had my meals at a separate small table. In the same room, though. I could see that they were eating much more and much better than I was, which I thought was unfair. The employment officer called round to make sure everything was as it should be. He asked me if everything was alright. I mentioned the meals. I could have been in a lot of trouble for complaining; after all, I'd seen a Ukrainian boy strung up from a tree nearby for being a troublemaker, but it didn't seem fair that I had so much less to eat and not even a cake, that they so enjoyed, to round it off. After all, I was working so hard on the farm ...'

When it was a merry or happy story, Michael would not intrude with laughter or even a shy chuckle. If it was a sad or mean story of wrongs done or hardship caused, Michael did not intervene with thoughts of self-pity. The stories almost came out as if they were neutral, as if these things had happened to someone else, for, in Michael's world, things simply happened, and it was for others to understand what emotions these things might arouse. The storyteller sought no sympathy, no pity, and no praise. It was a life that had been lived, simple as that. Through a war, through the loss to him of his entire family at home, through a displaced-persons camp, through marriage and the birth of a son in camp, through migration to a place he had only ever vaguely heard of, through the creation of a decent Australian life, through the troubles that another war caused.

Nor did Michael ever speak of Joe's 'war' or Joe's 'accident' or the 'tragedy' that befell his oldest child's life. Whenever it needed to come into the story, it was always, invariably, 'when this thing happened to Joe'. I must have heard that formulation thousands of times. 'When this thing happened to Joe'. In Michael's life, things happened. The art of life, the responsibility, was to accept what had happened, and to work with what was provided.

School happened in Michael's early life — only in the mornings and only for a few years — but he learned to read and write, and his teachers, so he said, always thought that he was bright and could go further. Singing happened in Michael's life, and when he was in the hills shepherding his family's few cows as they grazed and he was singing, people in the village would stop and listen. Later, they would tell him that they had listened and would say that they had liked what they had heard. These things happened. It was the storyteller's job to say what had happened, not why or what it meant. It was the listener's job to add that aspect to the story.

Let me try, briefly, to set a scene as the storyteller might have done, although present-day life was certainly not in Michael's repertoire.

It was a big yard, stretching about 80 metres down to the bank of Prospect Creek, though you couldn't see the creek from the porch, because it was screened by an enormous, rambling macadamia tree. Near the tree stood a couple of sheds, now in disrepair, housing the mower and the garden tools. An empty former chook house stood to the side. There had once been several chooks and many eggs. Closer to the back porch was the Hills hoist on one side of a little path and the vegie patch on the other. There had been all manner of vegies when I first started visiting, but it was a pretty straggly affair now — onions, shallots, potatoes, and carrots. Pressing up against the back porch, on the side, was the garage, crammed with stuff in two rooms and a small cooking area at the entrance. It had been the family's first 'house' on this block in the early 1950s.

We are sitting on the porch, Michael and I, two Michaels, each with a beer on this hot afternoon, in companionable silence for a few minutes. The factory across the creek is making its usual bumping and grinding noises; from the train line, just a block away from the front of the house, we can hear the boom gates go down, the ringing of the bells, and the train's horn sounding as it approaches the crossing, a few hundred metres on its way to Fairfield station. Sydney's west, the home of the 'battlers', as Michael liked to think of himself.

Michael lights another cigarette, takes another sip of his beer, and resumes his story. 'Pop!' — the cry comes bellowing from inside the house. Part request, part order. 'Poor Joe', Michael would sigh, brought back with a crash from his Ukrainian village, and maybe that favourite story, quite heroic, of the family protecting the church bell, part of their church next door, from those who wished to steal it. 'Poor Joe', he would sigh again.

'I'll go', I'd say, getting to my feet. 'Stay there.' In through the large back room, past the little kitchen and dining table, past the second bedroom and bathroom, past the hall cupboard, past Joe's bedroom, with its high bed and rudimentary lifter, and on into 'Joe's room', opposite the main bedroom and next to the front door, originally intended as the living room.

Joe in his wheelchair, slumped at an angle, usually, the television blaring some nonsense in the early afternoon. 'Can I have a cigarette', he will say, 'and a cup of coffee?'

'Joe, you've just had a coffee, but I'll get you a fag. Come outside, though. We're having a beer, your dad and I. Come and have a yarn.' But he rarely did. He liked being inside. The television diverted him, but could he follow the story? And he kept his own company. 'Michalina will be back soon,' I'd say, 'and then she'll start on the dinner. Do you want to sit with her as she cooks?' Negative, he would say, and laugh. I would return to the storyteller once the fag had been lit, maybe with a fresh beer for both of us.

A World of Wars

This book attempts to look at the impact of war on a father and son across two of the biggest conflicts ever known: the Second World War and the war in Vietnam. Given the numbers of those killed in each of these conflicts, it may seem quirky, beyond reason, to concentrate on two men, and their families, to the exclusion of all else. We need to understand that war comes right down to the personal level and may affect families in ways they could never have anticipated.

During the first half of the 20th century, Europe was engulfed in brutal, savage, destructive war, twice, from 1914 to 1918 and again from 1939 to 1945. A period of long peace followed, but, as the century came to an end, savage war broke out once more, fuelled by centuries-old ethnic hatreds and passions. The causes of the two great European wars of the 20th century are not as easy to explain. In 1914, it seemed that Europe was just itching for a fight, prepared to fling army against army, navy against navy for little good reason. In the days before war broke out elsewhere, significant elements within Britain's Liberal government spoke against British involvement, but there were few other voices of reason in Europe. While numbers of dead are notoriously difficult to tally in wars of such vast scale, a useful guide would suggest that between 8.5 and 10.8 million soldiers, predominately from Europe, lost their lives in the four years of the 'Great War'. This pales into insignificance compared to the war that began in 1939 — it has been estimated that 60 million people, or 3 per cent of the world's total population, perished during those six years.

Those anticipating the coming of war a second time in Europe in 1939 expected devastation if not total annihilation. These fears centred on the sophistication of the world's new air forces and the extraordinary destructive capacity of the bombs their aircraft could now carry. Peoples in the rest of the world looked in horror at the damage to British cities, most famously London, in the Blitz that randomly struck at civilians of every station in life and every calling. The bombs killed babies, children, mothers, workers, socialites — anyone at all whose luck had expired.

Later, attention turned to the even greater destruction of German cities, targeted partly in retaliation for the bombing of Britain and partly in the hope that the German people would rise up against their leader, their Fuhrer, the insane Adolf Hitler, to bring his war to an end. This didn't happen, and British and American armies, moving from a westerly direction, and Russian troops, from the east, rushed across the defeated German homelands before capturing and nearly destroying its capital and most famous city, Berlin. Only then, in May 1945, did the fighting stop in Europe; only then could people feel safe from the massive nightly raids of the bombers. The devastation caused by the aerial bombardment from both sides might not have been as complete as people had feared in the 1930s, but it was, nevertheless, on a previously unimaginable scale.

None of the European nations except for France and the Soviet Union were involved in the Asian wars of the second part of the 20th century. The loss of life in these Asian wars was also horrendous, and the destruction from aerial bombardments with vastly more sophisticated aircraft and weaponry is frightening in its extent. Commentators liked to use measurements from the Second World War in describing the tonnage of bombs dropped on Vietnam or Cambodia, and seemed somewhat pleased to be able to say that Vietnam had more bombs raining down on it than Germany in the Second World War. Yet it had become clear, at least by 1975, that mass warfare conducted by the world's industrialised powers could possibly bring about the end of human life on this planet. This didn't stop the recourse to warfare in more localised settings, but worldwide warfare has, thankfully, been avoided.

War stories come to us in unusual ways. I seem unable to write about the grand strategies, the big battalions, the overall shape and meaning of enormous battlefields and armies. For me, war has always come down to the individual, as this book will show. I have a friend of many years who recently shared with me his own story — of which, to this point, I had been entirely ignorant. My friend's parents had made their home in Ardleigh Green in Essex, close to the English coast and also close to London. In 1944, the Germans had begun sending their V1 rockets to London and were causing awful and extensive destruction, much worse than anything the bombers had done three years earlier. With sophisticated double-agent trickery, the British managed to convince the Germans that the rockets were overflying London by about 20 miles. The Germans adjusted their rockets accordingly, which meant that they rained down on Essex, causing far less damage than if they had fallen in central London. My friend was not yet born; his mother was expecting her confinement in about five months' time; she was having twins. A massive V1 explosion near his parents' house catapulted my friend's mother from the chair in which she had been sitting and sent her across the room, crashing to the floor. She lost one of her twins at this moment, but carried both babies to full term; my friend, obviously, survived. This is war at its most random and most intimate. In this book, I will be writing not about that English family, but of a family where not one generation, but three, were caught up in the awful evil of war. For them, too, war was random and totally life-changing.

The first man to go to war in the 20th century from the Stawyskyj family was Stefan Stawyskyj, Michael's father, who fought in the armies of the Austro-Hungarian Empire for almost the entire length of the war of 1914–1918. I do not know very much at all about his service and would like to know more. I do know that he fought on the Yugoslav front, that he was wounded in action, and that his war service caused him a lifelong disability. As Stefan died in the early-to-mid-1940s, it's fair to assume that his early death may have been linked to his war service. Stefan was a Ukrainian peasant boy when he left for war and was almost certainly conscripted into the army that he joined. His son and his grandson would both serve in wars as conscripts. While we know a great deal more about their experience of war, I am reluctant to leave Stefan's experience of war out of this account altogether. His service, and its consequences, should be acknowledged and remembered. However, this book will of necessity focus on the stories of Michael and Joe.

Some would say that leaders should know the likely consequences of their actions before they choose war over peace. Europe may have gone to war somewhat unknowingly in 1914. It suffered no such blindness in 1939, as the victims of the earlier war and the consequences of the awful loss of life were everywhere to be seen, still. If Chamberlain ashamed many of his fellow countrymen with his craven capitulation to Hitler at Munich in 1938 for 'peace in our time', should he really be blamed for that? Europe knew all about war by then and should have being doing everything possible to avoid it a second time. These are problems for philosophers as much as they are for historians, but the experiences of the Stawyskyj family will show you how intimate, personal, and arbitrary mass warfare can become. This is a painful tale, but it is a story of Europe and Australia at war.

Part One

MICHAEL'S STORY

The Village

MICHAEL STAWYSKYJ WAS BORN on 3 June 1922, in the village of Banyca. This seems a relatively simple statement, and I am very confident that the date is correct. But the new baby was not given the name Michael. That name would come some time later, tentatively in Germany and then permanently in Australia. The baby was baptised Mychajlo, probably unpronounceable in Australia. Almost every European document regarding Michael's life, even his application to settle in Australia, uses Mychajlo as his name, as would every family member in his early life and every villager among whom he grew up. The village, too, had a variety of spellings, including Banyzia and Banycia. Regardless of the variety of spellings, Banyca was a real village and Mychajlo was a real baby. I hope the reader will forgive me if I call the baby, young man, and grown man Michael throughout this story, as this was how I always knew him and how he named himself from his mid-20s onwards.

The village is now on the Polish side of the border and it was in Michael's time, too. To add to its confusions, the village name is now spelt Banica, though Michael's Ukrainian spelling must have been used at some stage in the village's history. Most of the people in the village in 1922 spoke Ukrainian. Michael would say that the nearest big city was Gribu (now Grybow), 40 kilometres away, yet the nearest city was Lvov, in Ukraine, 270 kilometres from Banyca. Lvov, when Michael was born, had a population of 219,000 people, and thus can fairly be called a city; Gribu, even today, has only 12,400 people. We can say that Michael was not used to big cities and crowds of people. He described himself as of peasant background. But that was just a fact; it implied no value judgement at all.

Michael's father was Stefan Stawyskyj and his mother was Maria. He had two brothers, Stefan and Ivan (John in Australia), and two sisters, Ulaska and Anna; an older and a younger brother; an older and a younger sister. He was, he said, in the middle. Stefan was Maria's second husband; her first husband, and the father of Maria's first two children, had died. Michael thought of himself as and, indeed, was Ukrainian, 'because you'd been teached from parents when you were born [that you were Ukrainian] … and you first learn Ukrainian language'. Statesmen might draw and redraw national boundaries, but ordinary folk knew who they were.

Michael's parents owned a farm, which Maria had inherited from her first husband, 'but a very small one', in Michael's words. What does that mean? About ten hectares or so, he thought (about 25 acres). His father grew vegetables on the farm, onions and potatoes, almost solely for the family's own use. Michael's parents were not wealthy people and there was little money ('there was no way to make money, you know, in those days'), but there was enough food ('we have enough because we produce everything on the farm what we needed'). They had some cows and horses, but, again, I can't tell you the extent of the stock, though I suspect there were very few animals.

The family lived in a wooden house in the village, with very thick walls to keep out the cold. Nice big rooms, Michael remembered, but not many of them. Michael slept with his brothers and sisters. The village was in a valley, surrounded by mountains, and there might have been about 90 houses in the village, probably most made of wood, like his own. It was very cold in the village in winter, but Michael remembered the summers with pleasure and real joy. There were no shops in his village, though there were a few in one nearby. There was a school, 'of course', which Michael attended from the age of seven for five years or so. But only in the morning, from 8.30 until one o'clock. After that, it was farm work.

What did Michael learn at school? Well, Polish for one thing, because that was the language of instruction. He learned Ukrainian at home and a little bit at school, to read and write his own language. There was a little bit of mathematics, too, he remembered, how to add up. Michael was proud of his work at school, and his teacher clearly thought well of him. He was attentive and clever. He could pick up the reading aloud whenever asked, and he already had a fine singing voice. One of his teachers (the only teacher?) thought he might continue his education by going to study for the priesthood, the only way a poor peasant boy might go further in life, but that was out of the question. He was needed on the farm. Even late in his life, Michael remembered his school days with pleasure and some pride. He liked to say that he was good at school. It helped to define him. He was not just a farm boy.

One of the teachers whom he remembered was a rather stern woman, eager to discipline naughty little boys. In the winter, the boys would climb a low hill near the school and slide down the hill on their bottoms. This, of course, would make their pants very wet, and there would be plenty of smacks on those damp bottoms for boys who came into class with wet pants. There were no uniforms at school and children wore what they wore at home. In summer, everyone went to school barefoot, but there were boots for winter. There was little time for games, Michael remembered, but he would have liked to have had a go at soccer. There was only one problem: nobody had a ball.

I asked Michael if he had studied geography at school, and he said he had, a little. I asked him if he had ever come across Australia at school, and he said that he hadn't. And then came a memory that perhaps he had forgotten for many years. There was a book, he said, that they read in grade three, which showed an Australian Aborigine 'throwing boomerang on the dirt'. But where Australia was, or anything else about it, was not something they were giving attention to in Ukrainian/Polish schools in those years.

School, and then, of course, church. Every Sunday from ten in the morning until about noon (the Ukrainian Catholic liturgy is much more complicated and thus lengthier than the ordinary Roman-Rite Catholic Mass). Then there was another church service at four in the afternoon, which the family always attended, perhaps some type of Benediction service. The Ukrainian liturgy is sung, and Michael remembered with considerable affection the singing of all the people in the church, for the services in Ukraine were in Ukrainian, while the rest of the Catholic world still struggled under the intolerable burden of Latin. It was a big church building, wooden again, put up by the village people. The priest, when Michael was a little boy, was very old and had spent all his life in the village. He was almost certainly married, as Ukrainian Catholic priests can be, and probably participated fully in village life. After his death or retirement, new and younger priests came, but rarely lasted more than a couple of years in Banyca.

There was turmoil when Michael was about 15 years of age, because Ukrainian Orthodox people came to the village to poach souls. Up to that point, everyone had been Catholic and everyone, naturally, attended church. But then 'some people come from somewhere and start teaching [the people] about Ukrainians are supposed to be all Orthodox, and part went there, and part stayed with the same church. They build another church then for Orthodox church. There was lots of trouble because they start fighting each other.'

Michael's family was in the thick of it. His parents stayed loyal to the old church, which was either next door to their own house or very close by. The Orthodox push must have been quite successful, and, before long, the Orthodox Christians accounted for a majority of the people in the village. So they said, in triumph, we should have the church bell (a very valuable and important item) now that we have the greater number of adherents — and, as you might expect, the Catholics were having none of that. Michael, his father, and his older brother were now on 'bell watch', looking out each night for a gang of marauders intent on pinching the bell, and fighting them off. And it did come to that; they would ring the bell when the Orthodox men approached, as a way of calling out the Catholic defenders. To the best of my knowledge, the bell stayed Catholic. Michael rejoiced in a job well done.

It was tough to be born into the world anywhere in 1922, but particularly in Europe. As a young boy, Michael observed the effects of the economic crisis the whole world knew as the Great Depression. He saw the rise of racial hatred, of evil ideologies, and the prospect of war, which, in all likelihood, might draw him into the fighting. Michael couldn't see a life for himself on the family farm — there wasn't enough work for three fit men, though there had been plenty of work for an eager little boy. But it 'was very hard to get job' elsewhere. 'It was very hard. Usually, Polish government in these days said, "If you want a job, you should be Polish."' A border might have made you Polish, but your own people and the government knew that you were Ukrainian, and you were worse off for that.

There was no work for people in the village. Some went to America and some came back, 'but they didn't last long and went back again'. While at home, they spoke of a world Michael could only dream about: 'people have cars and things like that … we usually didn't believe it'. In Banyca, people 'just work on the farms and grow things so they can feed themselves'. Michael's mother tried to sell her surplus eggs, but no one had the money to buy them.

It was possibly unusual that Michael's mother, Maria, owned the family farm; her husband, Stefan, had come from a neighbouring village and had no land. Her parents were, most likely, landless peasants, too, though Michael had never known her father, for he was dead. Maria's mother still lived in the village when Michael was a little boy, and there were no grandparents from his father's side. His father, Stefan, had fought in the First World War, in the Austrian army. He had been wounded, shot in the arm, which Michael said had caused that arm to be two inches shorter than the good arm. There was a small pension to compensate for this wound, very small I would think. Stefan had had no training as a soldier and was simply taken from his village for the war. Michael thought he had fought 'somewhere near Yugoslavia' and that he had been in the army for almost the full four years.

Army life figured on Michael's horizon, too, as a Polish citizen. Each young man, when he turned 21, was required to serve for 18 months in the Polish army, 'if you are fit'. His brother Stefan had started his period of service, but sustained an injury of some kind 'and they let him go home again'. This would tell us that Stefan was quite a deal older than Michael, at least five years or so. By the time Michael turned 21, the Polish army no longer existed, having been destroyed by the might of the German army within weeks of the Second World War starting, leaving many of Stefan's co-conscriptionists likely dead on the battlefield. The chances of war.

Michael left school at the age of 14 and turned to full-time work on the farm. 'Of course, it was hard work', he said, and laughed at the thought of it. Everything had to be done by hand. Scything the grass for hay for the winter, scything the wheat and the oats, 'no tractors, no nothing'. Ploughing the land with a horse — 'that was easy' because the horse did most of the work. But the soil was not good, 'lots of little stones in the ground, being the mountains … not good for anything but potatoes'. So lots of potatoes were planted, and 'usually everybody go there [everybody in the family, that is] when you take it out potatoes.

Children pick it ...' You could try to sell the potatoes, 'but sometime didn't pay to bring into the market because so cheap'.

And after work ended for the day? 'You can go to see the friends ... In the summer, boys just go out walking and singing ... drinking, if you have money to buy something', but Michael was too young to drink. He didn't have a girlfriend, yet, he said forcefully, 'I was very happy ... If you healthy, so you happy.' Michael was healthy; he had never seen a doctor. Indeed, there wasn't a doctor for at least 25 kilometres.

Michael used to come to stay with us in Canberra in the last part of his life, though he didn't like it very much, because he hated to be away from his own home. I would drive him down to the Tuggeranong valley, where there was a club where we could spend some quiet time together. It was almost always the same as we swung out of our suburb and drove further down the valley. Michael would then see our mountains, the Brindabellas, which fringe southern Canberra. Beautiful blue-green mountains, dominating our low settled plains. And his heart would stir as he saw them and he would be happy again. He was a mountain man. Canberra's mountains reminded him so powerfully of home. Of where he had roamed minding the family's cows as a little boy. Of where he had roamed with his friends in the long summer twilight, singing their lungs out, in the joy of the mountains, the valley, the village, and home.

When he was out with the cows, he would sing to them with his strong, powerful, and surprisingly deep voice for the sheer joy of it all. When he came back into the village, the people would tell him that they had heard him up there, making his songs, making them smile to hear him. 'You didn't know any better life, you know ... If you healthy, so you happy.'

War Comes

THERE WERE NO RADIOS in Banyca and no newspapers. Yet, somehow, the village people kept up with at least some of the news. People travelled from village to village passing on what they had heard. Perhaps the priest was a little better informed than most and told his parishioners what he knew. Perhaps it was hard to suppress the news of the awfulness that was engulfing their homes, villages, and nations at the command of Hitler. Around the world, people watched in newsreel cinemas as his unfolding madness developed; they heard his remarkable speeches on the radio; they read in the newspapers as western leaders ducked and weaved, trying to appease him. The people of Banyca and the other villagers of Poland and Ukraine were spared the details of all these things and had only the vaguest knowledge of the way the world was. But they would feel its consequences in much the same strength as people elsewhere in Europe. Except that they might be spared the bombing.

How much did Michael Stawyskyj know about the coming approach of war? Did he and his friends in the village talk about it and what it would mean for them? You would expect so. To have turned 17 exactly three months before war was declared on 3 September 1939 was the worst possible timing. No such young European boy could think that the war would not affect him. Most of these young Europeans would have thought that they would soon be in an army, and many might have thrilled at this thought. For some, there was the dream of the glory of defending, or expanding, the homeland; of performing brave and remarkable feats; of the advantage of a uniform, to become a recognised and visible part of the military, esteemed by generations of preachers, poets, statesmen, and other mythologisers.

Michael might have recognised quite early on, even before the war broke out, that the world he had known of family farm, of church, of friends, of village life must be coming to an end. But he couldn't have known that, on leaving his parents for the first time, he would never see them again. That, in saying goodbye to his mother, he would never again speak to her face-to-face. That he would never again be able to go to his father for the kind of advice a young man needs: to discuss his plans, to talk about marriage when the time came, to talk together about approaching manhood. He could not have known, either, that he would never again set eyes on the bed he had slept in all his life; that he would never again sit in the kitchen with his family, where he had taken almost all his meals and spent almost all of his winter evenings. He could not have known that he would never again enter the church where he had prayed since earliest childhood. That he would never again walk in the mountains that he had so loved. War would rob Michael Stawyskyj of all this.

Within two weeks of the opening of the war, troops arrived in Banyca to institute a new world order. But it was not the German army in the first instance that marched into Banyca. Instead, perhaps to general surprise, it was elements of the Slovakian army that arrived. I must admit that I was surprised and sceptical when Michael told me this. The Slovakian army, not the German army? Can that be right? A good test, perhaps, for the reliability of Michael's memory of events so long ago. But you'd think, too, that an event so momentous as this, so remarkable in this quiet village, so earth-shattering, would stick in the memory. The Slovakian army, now that's a surprise. Unless you had been following world events. In that case, you would have to have known that Slovakia, a minnow in Europe, had allied itself with Germany — for simple reasons of survival.

On 14 March 1939, Hitler, as a part of his intended destruction of Czecho-Slovakia, had created a puppet Slovak state. The Slovak parliament, on that date, declared its independence from Czecho-Slovakia and its alignment with Germany, and seemed to be acting as an independent emerging nation. Nonsense, of course; the whole sham in Bratislava had been orchestrated in Berlin, with the Slovak president and parliamentarians bit players in the drama. The parliamentary declaration of independence had, in fact, been drafted in Berlin. Slovakia became a part, in all but name, of the German Reich. When Hitler invaded Poland, the new Slovak republic 'generously' contributed a number of infantry and artillery battalions. It's not improbable that some of these troops found themselves in Banyca; perhaps they had been in the region even earlier. Michael's memory was clear about what he saw in the first days of the war, and certainly plausible.

But there were Germans, also, before long. Little changed in the village at first. The money was the same, the mayor kept his job. The Germans merely told the mayor what was expected of the village and its people: 'if the people didn't obey, then they [the Germans] come and punish them'. Were they taking food from the people? Not at this stage. The Germans recognised, or so Michael believed, that the people were too poor to be able to give up their own food, and perhaps there was an element of trying to win 'hearts and minds' in this. Or not. They wouldn't take the food, but they would take some of the villagers themselves. 'They just come in the village and told the mayor that where's three men in a house, one have to go to work in Germany.' Who could know what that meant, then, to 'work in Germany'. Work for wages? Look for work yourself, in a factory or on a farm that suited you, with the prospect of trips back home for holidays, and the normal passing to and fro between work life and home life? Who could know?

There were three men in Michael's house. Michael's father had already served in an army in war and had been wounded. Michael's elder brother, Stefan, had already been released, early, from his conscription obligations with the Polish army for some undisclosed reason. But Stefan's problem must have been serious enough, because armies don't easily let go of their conscripts. In a system where every male had to serve, only a serious matter would earn the conscript early release. So we can assume Stefan simply wasn't eligible for this new draft. That left Michael, the third man in this peasant home, if a boy of 17 can be called a man.

Artists, European artists particularly, have long loved to linger on the scene where a man leaves the family home to go off to the army. I was wandering through the Belvedere palace in Vienna, with its rich collection of paintings and other artworks, knowing that I would have to write soon the scene where Michael Stawyskyj leaves his family. I came across an 1813 painting by Johann Peter Krafft (1780–1856) *Der Abschied des Landwehrmannes* ('the departure of the territorial-army man') as just one example of this frequently painted scene. A uniformed man is holding the hand of a woman, his wife we presume, and she is holding a baby in her other arm. Two older children, a four-year-old and a five-year-old, look on; their gaze tells us they are much saddened to be losing their father. An older man (grandfather?) clasps his hands in prayer and looks heavenwards, while a younger woman (sister?) sits on a stool, her head in her hands, apparently weeping. A soldier behind the departing man seems to be hurrying on the issue. Through a partly opened door, in the background, we glimpse a large body of soldiers. It's a scene of sadness and poignancy.

And so to Michael's scene. As a much younger man, he's not leaving behind a wife and children. There's no grandfather. But there are sisters and a much younger brother, who can take the part of those weeping and saddened young participants. In Michael's scene, we add a mother and a father. A mother who must have known war before, as a child; a mother surrendering a son to war for the first time ever in her life. A father who knows war intimately from four years' service and from a tough wound that remained with him still. A father who knew of orders and discipline, of the loss of freedom to say how he would live his life and what he would do; who knew of wretched conditions, of cold, of mud and misery. Who was now surrendering his son to possibly all of that. His son, who had volunteered to take the father's place in an outburst of generosity and love. A son who might have stayed.

Michael was matter-of-fact about all this in his storytelling, downplaying his own bravery and generosity. 'My father want to go and leave me home, but he was not in very good health, so I decided to.' Had there been an argument over this, had there been intense family discussion and conference? Or had it been done in the presence of a demanding German soldier ordering an instant decision and immediate departure? Had there been time for consideration and careful thought, or was it done at the point of a rifle with harsh shouts and bad temper? My memory of the storyteller and his description of this important scene in his life is of an almost instant departure, with little time for argument or discussion. That's how I think it went. Yet there had been an order given to the mayor, which might have taken a few days to implement. Whatever of that, Michael had stood up as a man, to take on the burden of his family's contribution to Germany's war, and had taken the burden from his father and his elder brother. You packed up your clothes, I asked him. 'Oh, not many clothes', he said, and laughed.

And then he said his goodbyes. To his brothers. To his sisters. To his mother and father. A slight young man, but strong and fit, doing a duty to his family for who knew how long. The shape of the world was so unclear at this moment. What little news this family had gave no clue to Michael's likely fate and the length of his absence from the family home. Would it be mere months, as his father might have thought 25 years earlier when he first went to war, or would it be years, as his father's service had turned out to be?

The war had yet barely begun, and this time is now known in British and French history books as the 'phoney war' period. There was not too much phoney about the war in the east, however. Hitler had smashed and grabbed where and what he could, and had concluded a non-aggression treaty with Soviet Russia. No one could say with any conviction how it would all play out in the west, but most issues in the east seemed settled, unless the Russians had a change of heart. Stalin, the Russian tyrant, had huge armies at his command, which he might at some stage employ against Hitler. But not yet.

Perhaps the war was destined to last only a few weeks or months. Perhaps the Germans would stare down the western European powers once more and negotiate another peace with them. Could the world be mad enough to plunge itself into a lengthy war again, just 20 years since the last one had been concluded? Surely there must be reason for some hope? Take my boy, his mother might have been thinking, but send him back to me when you have sorted all this madness out. Would Michael be home in a matter of months? Who could possibly say? But a mother would fear the worst as she watched in these strained circumstances as her second son climbed into the truck that would take him — you and I know, forever — away from his home and his village.

First to the doctors, 'and if you have no disease or anything, they just put you on the trains'. Michael was fit and healthy (was this his first appearance before a doctor?), and, soon, with other Ukrainian boys, he was on his way to Germany. What did they talk of, as the train raced across the early winter countryside? How could they know what the future might hold? 'If you healthy, so you happy.' Please let it be so.

Zivilarbeiter

WARS ARE WON BY the big battalions. Wellington, with his allied armies, outnumbered Napoleon at Waterloo and had a smashing victory. When Americans began to arrive on the Western Front in late 1917, the game was up for the German army, as its 'black day' would soon show. Indeed, in fear of the massing numbers, the Germans attempted their near-successful breakout in March 1918. They knew they needed to move quickly, before the big battalions arrived.

It was a lesson well learned, even if it did not quite work then. The Germans knew they needed an army of technical skill and superiority, of course, but of numbers, too. They also remembered the awful fate of the people at home in the final period of the last war. Shortages of everything — of food, of farm produce, of war materiel. Factories and farms stripped of labour to push every male, even boys, into a dwindling army, the home front at near collapse, and people at the point of insurrection in the face of their great sufferings. A second time around, things must be different.

So it was determined that the conquered peoples from all around the German empire would provide the labour that had been in such short supply last time. There were several categories of such workers across the six years of this long war. Some, the 'undesirables', were placed in forced-labour camps and would be worked until they died, on short rations and in desperate conditions, and if they could not work they would be killed. Among the 'undesirables' were Jews, of course, and criminals, homosexuals, the homeless, political and religious dissidents, and communists.

Others in camps, in increasing numbers as the war progressed, were prisoners of war, captured on the battlefields, all, except the officers, forced to work. The Russian prisoners were treated with terrible cruelty, but the others in this category were, possibly, the best-treated workers, for whom the Germans respected the application of the Geneva Convention and allowed their camps to be inspected by the International Red Cross. Western prisoners of war were also protected to the extent that the Germans understood that their own prisoners in the hands of the British or the Americans might be subjected to retaliation if reports from Germany were too bad.

Suffering as intensely as the Russian prisoners of war were the 'ostarbeiter' — that is, civilian conscripts from the east, principally from Ukraine, who were treated with depraved ferocity. Held in camps with barbed wire and under guard, they largely worked in factories in appalling conditions. They were malnourished, worked long hours, and were treated with complete indifference. Many of these workers died.

Finally, there were the 'zivilarbeiter', primarily from Poland, who did not live in camps, in general, and often worked on farms or in the houses of Nazi and civilian officials at the decree of a labour-management officer. They had few privileges and were treated far below the standards given to German workers in the same jobs, but they were not treated with contempt or inflamed cruelty. They were paid some kind of a wage, however low, though most of it went in food and housing. What remained was of little value: they were given no holidays and were expected to work all seven days each week; and they couldn't own things of any value, such as bicycles or cameras. They weren't allowed to use public transport — indeed, they were not allowed freedom of movement. They could not attend German church services, or enter restaurants or swimming pools, public parks, museums, galleries, and the like, if any of these were available in the villages and towns in which they found themselves. By 1944, there were about 7.8 million of these zivilarbeiter workers. Big battalions indeed.

Foreign workers were specifically prevented from fraternising with the host population, though friendships must have arisen among those working on small farms, for example. The German authorities repeatedly issued instructions and pamphlets specifically warning of the dangers of such friendships to the health and wellbeing of the German state. Sexual relations between Germans and foreign workers were absolutely forbidden, resulting in the execution of the foreigner and the imprisonment of the German for those who broke the rules. But physical attraction would have arisen between young farm boys and German women, often lonely in the absence of their own menfolk. Everyone recognised that such attraction was very dangerous indeed.

Those in the camps, except western prisoners, were the horrendous victims of an evil ideology. It was expected that most of them would die. Zivilarbeiter workers fared somewhat better. They would be fed and clothed, and they would live in normal civilian conditions, in a house with a bed of their own, though the house might be crowded. There might be friendship and respect shown to them. Nevertheless, they were slaves in the usual meaning of that term. They were not free to come and go from their jobs or to determine where, at what, and how long they would work. If they were not actually the property of the individual farmer or housekeeper who housed and employed them, they were, in a sense, the property of the state. They were subject to orders at all time and would be punished if they transgressed. Punishments ranged from beatings, to imprisonment, to execution. They were slaves and would remain so until the state released them from their servitude, whenever that might be.

Farm Boy in Germany

WAR HAD COME SLOWLY to Europe this time, unlike the impulsive rush in 1914. When had it started its creep? People disagree. But by 1938, it was coming, everyone could see that, for who could appease the German chancellor, Adolf Hitler, in his ferocious push for more people, more territory, a greater Germany? Now he was threatening war over his push for Sudetenland, which was, since 1919, a part of Czecho-Slovakia.

Negotiate and appease, back off from confrontation, work and pray for 'peace in our time' was the mantra in the west. It amounted to peace at any price. Hitler insisted that the German people should all live in one nation, one 'reich', and he blustered and fought for this objective. There were German people in Czecho-Slovakia, he screamed and ranted, who must become 'ein volk'. 'Ein Volk, ein Reich, ein Fuhrer', he bellowed: one people, one empire, one leader. Perhaps a quarter of all the people in Czecho-Slovakia were German in racial origin, and many of these people lived close to the border with Germany, in the Sudetes mountain region, an area with over 50 per cent German population. Hitler demanded the 'return' of Sudetenland (formerly part of the Austro-Hungarian Empire) to Germany. British prime minister Neville Chamberlain and the other appeasers gave Hitler what he wanted. But it wasn't enough, this swallowing up of Sudetenland — Hitler demanded more and more, and, finally, war came. But Sudetenland, for now, was German.

The trains taking Polish men from their homes to their slavery stopped first in Germany, at Dresden, near the Polish border. There, the men were fed. 'Was not bad', said Michael, remembering how he had looked in wonder at his first glimpses of wartime Germany. He did not speak any German, and it must have been hard, a foreigner listening to this strange language, men barking orders at him and his mates, with them only understanding the general intention. Then waiting for hours, days possibly, for allocation to work, and then more travel, this time to the farms on the border, the farms of Sudetenland. Lucky to be classified as zivilarbeiter rather than ostarbeiter, though he couldn't know it.

Michael went to a small farm in Sudetenland, not unlike the small farm from which he had just been taken, 'nearly seem like home, you know'. Potatoes as the staple crop, a few animals, mountains surrounding the farm. The family there, being Germans, 'manage to live a bit better than we did', but the situation was familiar and not too threatening. Hard work, though, 12 to 14 hours a day. Like at home, it was planting and picking, shepherding and feeding, all manual labour, horses not tractors, scythes not machines. Michael lived in the farmhouse with the family: a man, his wife, and one daughter. He had a space at the top of the house, in the attic, and 'quite a good bed'. At first, he ate with the family, and ate what they ate, which was the peasant food he had been used to, but perhaps there was just a little bit more and it was a little bit better. When he wasn't working, Michael would meet up with other Ukrainian boys working in the district: 'we go together and talk a little bit or something'. But not in a pub or inn, or, indeed, in any place where Germans might be. Perhaps just a barn or a shed, somewhere on one of the farms. There were plenty of police about, but few soldiers; the war, for what it was at this stage, was a long way away.

How was the war going, Michael might have wondered, and how long will we all be here? There was a radio in the farmhouse and everyone could hear Hitler telling the people what he wanted them to know. 'I didn't know what was Hitler. Hitler, you know, is Fuhrer, what you call him. You have to keep your mouth shut and that's all.' Did the Ukrainian boys open up on Hitler, on the German people, on their own lives, when they were alone together? Perhaps that might have been too dangerous, perhaps someone might hear and accuse them of plotting. And all those police about.

Sounds alright, all of this, at least in the context of a world at war. Michael was working hard, learning German quickly — he was always good with languages. He was sleeping soundly in a bed, eating what the family was eating. The employment man would call round to check on everything; that was his job. Michael came to know him and to like him. The boys talked about him, too; he was alright. He might be trusted. 'There was a very good man in employment ...' How lucky was that? A fair man, perhaps, and sympathetic.

Michael complained to the employment man about working on Sundays. He was a Catholic, he said, and the priests had said this was wrong, to work on Sundays. The employment man took his side: yes, there should be some rest, if not the whole day off. And so it was. Then the employment man came to the farm and asked Michael to come with him to another farm. There was a Ukrainian boy there who would not work, please talk with him, he can't refuse to work, it will be very bad for him. Michael did his best. He pointed out that they all must work; he pleaded with him to get up and work, 'don't you see what will happen', he said. But this boy had simply lost it. He would walk home, he said, he wanted to see his home and his family again. He didn't want to work for Germans, to take their orders and do their bidding. He would not work; he would go home. Michael tried as hard as he could, pleading, hoping the boy would see reason. But he failed. This Ukrainian boy was shot where he lay, in the barn, by the police, but Michael had gone by then, taken back to his own farm by the employment man. And they would have talked about that, at length, the Ukrainian boys, the punishment for not obeying, the consequences of doing the wrong thing. 'You have to be careful to say wrong word or something, or do something wrong, you know, but usually was quiet on the farm. If you be lucky to get good people, you have not a bad life, but you didn't learn anything, just work and work.'

Michael was on this first farm for a year, and then, in his words, he started a fight when conditions deteriorated. 'They been very tight with the money and everything ... I complained about bad food.' Now that was brave, and the food must have been pretty awful to risk such trouble. But, again, the employment man took Michael's side. Michael watched what the family ate and compared it with his own food, for they were now at separate tables. They now had richer food and more of it, and yet Michael was now doing most of the work. He was willing, he was trained, he knew what was expected, but these slops, he would complain. The employment man looked into the complaint. Yes, he was fair and sympathetic, perhaps a father himself, and Michael was a person easy to like, that was clear — honest, joyful, talkative, a good singing voice, good to be around. It seems that the employment man certainly took a liking to him, and, instead of ordering a beating, as he might have, he told the farmer's wife that Michael should be given exactly the same food as the family was eating. No separate servings, no second-class slops. And the farmer's wife didn't like it one bit; was Michael supposed to eat exactly the same as what her own daughter was eating? At the next meal, she piled Michael's plate up, but she was far from happy. Weren't these people different? Weren't they forbidden to mix with us as equals, couldn't we tell them what to do and when to do it? So the employment man moved Michael from this farm. 'There was employment office there in the town, and you go there and complain. If you was right, they listen to you. So he listened to me. He give me another job.'

To an even better billet and even more agreeable work. It 'was not a farm ... only two cows and one horse, and the man was very good to me because he was in the First World War for five years in Russian prison'. This man knew what it was like to be in another country, to work as a slave, to be treated as beneath contempt. He had suffered all this himself, and he would treat this young Ukrainian lad well; there had been too much suffering already. The man traded in firewood. He would buy it from the forest, take it to his own place, and chop it up even smaller, then sell it to the people in town. Wood to get a fire started, to give it a bit of a boost in this predominately coal area. 'It was very good food' at this new billet, and 'not too much work'.

Michael, with his horse and cart, would pick up the cut firewood in the forest, take it to his boss's place, unload the wood, and, with a circular saw, cut it smaller, then reload the cart and take the wood to the people's houses in town. It seems like a fair bit of work to me, but — with Michael on his cart for periods, out and about and meeting people, seeing new places all the time — this was a change for the very much better. He was on his own, largely, because his boss couldn't work: 'he was a little bit crippled, you know'. Possibly from his years in the Russian prison. So Michael was meeting townspeople every day, going into their houses to unload the wood, talking with them, maybe enjoying a coffee or a bit of food; 'they been very good'. Was he getting a better grip on the language? 'I already speak quite good, you know. And there's a lot of books [at] the top of his house, on the ceiling, you know, and I read a lot of books in German and I improve my language.' Good food? 'Terrific. Never been fed so good before.'

The boss had a wife and a daughter, again, and the daughter was about 30 years of age. She did the cooking in the home, and she looked after the two cows, milking them. Michael looked after the horse and delivered firewood twice a day. It was only a small village where he lived, about 15 houses, and there were no other Ukrainian boys in the village, but there were some in the next village, about five kilometres away, and he would go there from time to time, to talk his own language with them, to sing, and to play cards. They would talk about the war and who should win, but it was hard to know. 'I didn't know what to think, because German was not good for us and Russia was communist and worse.'

You didn't talk about the war with German people, 'the family where you were working, no', because they, of course, saw things differently. Michael's boss had two sons in the war, one of whom lost both his legs fighting somewhere. He came home and was given work in a nearby village as a postmaster; at least he'd survived. Michael recognised that the people he knew, the people with whom he lived, the people to whom he delivered the firewood were suffering; he saw their grief and he understood their anxiety for their country, their people, their family at war. So he learned not to talk about it with them; he really didn't need to stir these people up.

Then the second son came home, out of the army, too, another casualty. He must have been less badly wounded than his elder brother — he had a 30 per cent invalidity, whatever that meant — and his father gave him work with Michael in the forest. Now there were two carts, two horses, and two men. They were about the same age, these two men, and looked a lot like each other; indeed, 'people didn't recognise who is him, who is me from 30 yards away'. But they started fighting, the boss's son and the boss's worker, no brotherly love here. This was dangerous for Michael, a slave raising his hand against the young master. Why then? 'He was a very heavy smoker and it was already hard to get cigarettes. When he didn't have anything to smoke, he went mad.' And took it out on Michael, who stood up for himself.

So, after a year at what had been a very good billet, Michael went back to the employment man and told him how things had unravelled. Again, Michael found sympathy where there might have been a beating and an order to just get on with it. The employment man, instead, found Michael another job. His old boss was very sorry to see Michael go, and so was his wife. 'She was already an old woman, you know [probably in her 50s]. She was cooking, she put food in my bags when I was leaving. I didn't want to take it, and she said, "Better take it, you don't know where you end up."' A year Michael had been there, a good worker, almost a son to these two kindly Germans, but now he was on his way once more into unknown territory. Wiser after two years working in Germany, with good language skills and good work habits, Michael was surely an asset to any employer to whom he might be offered.

His thoughts were often of home. He exchanged letters with his family to keep up with the news, and he talked of home, of all their homes, with his Ukrainian mates. Of what his sisters were doing, of his younger brother and how the burden of the family farm was falling more heavily on him, of his father becoming increasingly unwell. That was a worry, but what could he do? Then, in 1943, his family told him that his father had died; they wrote of the funeral that he could not have gone to, of how they would cope and wait for him to come back home. That hit hard, to have his father die without Michael able to say goodbye, to miss the funeral and the elaborate Ukrainian liturgy, to think of the gravesite within the village cemetery, but not to be there to help his mother, his sisters, and his little brother. Homesickness was always there, but it hit hardest at times of crisis.

The next farm was about 18 kilometres away from his previous billet, so this was a real upheaval because Michael had not only lost a good position, he had also lost the company of his mates. The new place was a much bigger farm, with more fields, and several cows kept in the stalls all year round — which meant you had to feed them constantly, and clean up all the time. Much more work. The place did not have a good reputation, either. There'd been a Ukrainian boy working there before

Michael arrived who had been constantly in trouble and seemed to have been beaten up by the police about every two weeks. The farmer and his wife also housed their daughter-in-law, who worked in a nearby town and fought with her father-in-law because he wanted her to work on the farm. Somehow, the poor Ukrainian lad was caught up in the family's bad blood and they all took it out on him and reported him to the police. Michael learned from this: 'I was not so silly to get mixed up in the family.'

There was another problem, with the daughter-in-law: 'she liked more me than I [liked her]'. Sexual relations, signs of affection even, were strictly forbidden between German women and zivilarbeiter boys. Yet this married woman in the house where Michael was living was clearly giving Michael indications of her affection for him. One day, he was going off to see his friends, and she said, 'Wait for me. I go with you and see my girlfriend.' So they walked off together, which was dangerous. Indeed, they walked to the orchard ('there was a big orchard'), and they should not have been there. They might have been seen; Michael might have been reported to the police. There might have been all sorts of trouble. Michael was a good-looking young man; she was a lonely young woman fighting with her husband's parents, frustrated, no doubt, with her husband far away. A recipe for trouble.

Then the husband returned to the farm. 'He was so scared if anybody pinch her' (his wife, that is) that he seems to have deliberately injured himself to get away from where he was working in a local prison. Now he was working about the farm and keeping a close eye on his wife. One day, the husband knocked off a bit early from his farm work and put the coffee on. Michael said to him, 'When I finish this, I wash my hands and I come and drink coffee.' The man had already asked his wife to join him and she had already said no, but, when she saw Michael draw up a chair and take his cup, she immediately came to the table and sat down, too. It was too obvious. 'When I come, she come and sit there. Oh, he went crazy.'

There was another story that Michael told that must have come from this period, but from before the husband had returned to work on the farm. He came home from his work at the prison one evening, unexpectedly, and knocked on the door. His wife, Michael said, came into Michael's room to give Michael a kiss before running to open the door for her husband. An edited story, perhaps. It might have been, more realistically, that the wife left Michael's room in haste and surprise to run to open the front door for the unexpected return of her husband. If so, this was very, very dangerous, with execution the penalty for the erring but innocent zivilarbeiter.

What if, to put it at its mildest, a jealous husband were to report to the police that the Ukrainian zivilarbeiter was making a play for his wife? It may seem innocent, all this, and somewhat trivial, if we overlook the possible intrusion into Michael's room, but even the most innocent explanation of the situation was real danger for a farm boy with no rights and no redress. He might have returned her interest even mildly, he might not; he knew it was silly to get mixed up with the family, but, should real trouble arise, no one would wait to listen to his side of the story. Worse, the jealous husband was eventually sent back to his workplace, and who knew what thoughts might fester there. Michael thought, 'he was not cranky with me. He was very cranky with his wife.' So back to the employment man to try for another farm, a safer place.

'I told them everything like it was, you know, never lied to him or anything.' And he was moved once more, to another farm, about three kilometres away, where he worked for about a year without incident or difficulty. Then Michael heard that there was a Ukrainian boy from his own village working at a place not very far away from where Michael was. What if the two of them — they must have been friends — could work together, how comforting that would be to both, almost like family. 'So I tried the Employment again, and he give me this job.' This was Michael's fifth place during the war: 'I think the man in

Employment somehow he like me, because nobody else change five times in five years.'

The new boss must have been quite wealthy, because he had two big houses, and three Ukrainians and one Yugoslav prisoner working for him. The job was a tough one, working in the forest, loading timber and taking the wood for use in the coalmines, presumably for the steam engines there, and for roof supports and other types of building. 'We knew everything what to do with the timber in the hills, in big mountain, and was good for us. We had two pair of horses and wagons, you know, and we go in the forest, load it, and bring to the coalmine. For a whole year, until the war ended.' Hard work, but steady. Two good mates working together, talking all the time of home and their village, of the war, of life after the war. Two others to work and live with, a new language to learn — Yugoslavian, that is — fair accommodation and food, a reasonable boss. And a sense that the war might be coming to an end.

Danger

MICHAEL WAS WATCHING, day and night, as massive numbers of aircraft flew over his workplace and his region on their way to important targets in Germany. It seemed the Allied aircraft owned the skies, because the Luftwaffe no longer had the capacity to attack the enemy and defend the Fatherland. The war was coming to an end, you could sense that, Michael thought, and the German people knew it, too, though they never talked about it. Life became more dangerous as the Allies advanced: 'they didn't bomb [my region] until close to the end of the war', which was now. 'The worst was aeroplanes, they come down very fast with machine guns, you know, they shoot on the trucks and horses and things. Every day you'd be in danger … you still bringing timber to the coalmines, and many times we have to stop in the middle of the road and run somewhere, hide … Everyone was scared … Just lie down in a trench somewhere.'

The talk with his mates became more serious and urgent. What to do in this new situation? Run away, possibly into the arms of the advancing Americans? But how would they be received by an army intent on other things? In any case, running away was dangerous, 'if they catch you, won't be worth it'. Yet the Germans among whom they lived were now less stable and less sure. Terrified themselves, they were more likely to take it out on the less fortunate, the foreigners: 'some people did revenge themselves, you know'. And still the Americans kept coming, and still the planes came swooping in and then shooting at random or at anything that moved. Was it best, then, to wait and take orders from the Germans, who had been giving all the orders for five years, or to strike out on their own? But if so, where would they go? Home, where the heart lay, or to the west, where there might be a new life, new hope?

There were about 40 of them in this Ukrainian group, 'boys and girls' as Michael thought of them, and, even for the storyteller, the story now becomes quite confused. Michael was close to the Czecho-Slovakian border, so why not abandon Sudetenland, where he had spent the entire war, why not leave Germany altogether and go somewhere that might be more accepting? Why not, indeed. And so they would go. They would leave the places that had become their homes, abandon the people for whom they had worked, and leap into insecurity and danger. Born near the Czecho-Slovakian border, Michael suggested to his group that they try to travel cross-country to their own homes and villages. But there was still a war on and this was extremely dangerous. They could easily be captured by the Germans, or the Russians for that matter.

There might have been safety in numbers, but it was a big group and was this the best way to travel? Then, in these tumultuous times, they ran into a group of Russian soldiers. Come to Prague, an officer said, and talk with us; after a while, he went away and came back with two soldiers with machine guns and took the whole group into a camp. First, the Russians wanted to find out what everyone had been doing during the war. Did they help the Germans? Were they against the Americans? Had they fought against the Germans in any way? Or were they, well, and the word was quick to be used — collaborators? And this interrogation took two and a half months. In camp, poorly fed, with no facilities. In terror. Then the Russians divided the group and took the girls away, onto a train, out of their lives.

Did you have a girlfriend, I asked Michael, not for the first time — and this time, in the memory of these sharp days, with the background of a long and happy marriage to Anna, whom he was yet to meet,

Michael at last admitted that, indeed, he did have a girlfriend and her name was Caterina. In fact, he said, she had been his girlfriend for the last two and a half years, and now they were separated. She was a Ukrainian girl, of course, coming from a place about 300 kilometres from where Michael had lived, and working in a village about ten kilometres from where Michael was working. Now she was taken from him and he was never to see her again or ever know what had become of her. Taken to a train and taken away with all the other Ukrainian women.

There is another version of this story, which Michael told us only towards the end of his life. I think the two versions are not incompatible, it's just that the second version is much more personal and intimate. In this version, as the war is coming to an end, Michael says to Caterina that, as soon as possible, they must begin to move west. If they come into the hands of the Russians, they will be treated as collaborators, he says, and they may suffer a long period in a concentration camp, or worse. Caterina agrees, but says that she cannot possibly think of starting a new life without saying goodbye to her mother; and she insists on this. So Michael, against his better judgement, agrees to try to strike out for home. They do well in their travels for a time until eventually they are sitting on a railway station, awaiting a change of trains. Russian soldiers approach them, asking for their papers, which they show. The Russians say to Michael, 'You come with us', and to Caterina, 'You can go on your way.' And so they are separated. Caterina says to Michael as he is led off, 'However long it takes, and wherever you are taken, I will wait for you.' And, as in the first version, they never see each other again, never hear from each other again; and, in this late revelation, Michael says to us how desperately he would like to know what had been her fate, her life.

However it was that they were separated, whether as a loving couple or as part of a bigger group, or a bit of both, frankly, Michael and his Ukrainian mates were now in a fair bit of trouble. They had no papers, no passports, or any documentation like that, because the Russians had confiscated everything. Indeed, the Russians seemed to believe that the Ukrainian slave workers had been living the good life in Germany, helping the German war effort, doing what they could to assist the Germans to win the war. So the Russians got Michael's group working, clearing out the mess of war, and here there was one stroke of extreme good fortune. All these Ukrainian boys had played cards for many hours during their time in Germany — it was one of the few pleasant things they could do. Now, in the camp, the boys were playing cards again, just for fun. A Russian officer came over and asked if he could join in and could they play for money. Michael had a few German marks, which he had held onto from somewhere, and the Russian agreed to take the marks on an exchange rate of 100 marks for one Czecho-Slovakian koruna. Michael couldn't stop winning. His mates soon dropped out, and it was only the Russian and Michael, and 'I won 3,000 korunas from him … I was thinking he would be cranky but he get up, he slap me on the shoulders as if to say "good boy".'

There is another version of this story, too, although, again, the basics are the same. In the second version, at the railway station, after he has been separated from Caterina, he plays cards with the Russian soldiers who have detained him. Again, he wins quite a lot of money. At one point, a Russian officer enters the room, sizes up the situation, and tells Michael to pick up his winnings and go straight away, 'otherwise they will kill you'. And he does as he is told, and uses some of the money to buy a train ticket west.

It is more likely that Michael won the money from the Russian officer in the camp. But memory is fallible. Perhaps there was more than one game of cards, as there had been so many games of cards with Michael's own friends earlier in the war. Possibly, in his memory, card-playing was a social activity, and he would rarely have played with just one other person. These were confused times, and it was not easy for Michael to recall with perfect clarity every step along the way. There certainly was a game of cards, however, and it certainly made a crucial difference in the course of Michael's life. It was a random moment of enormous importance, never to be forgotten.

The Russians then decided to move the group from the camp in which they were housed to who knew where. They would force the Ukrainians to walk a long distance from one camp to another, presumably further away from the advancing American armies and more securely into Russian-controlled territory. Michael had no idea where they were going, but the group suspected or had heard a rumour that they were off to somewhere near the Romanian border, just to get them out of the way. This was not a good prospect at all and possibly a very long walk. For some reason, probably for their own safety from air attack, they were marched along the roads during the night and rested during the day. One night, Michael and two of his mates simply detached themselves from the group and hid in a nearby field. There were so many homeless people on the move that a little party of three attracted almost no notice. Still, none of them had any papers and there was risk in everything. But Michael did have quite a lot of money.

They had become aware that there was some order returning to life in Germany as the Allies began to produce an appropriate civilian government, though run by the military. It was clear to them by now that Germany had been divided into four zones, the Russian, the British, the French, and the American. It was also clear that, in terms of the future, making for the American zone was by far the best idea. This would give them some access to American wealth and know-how, and some prospect, possibly, of eventual resettlement in the United States. So the idea now for Michael's much diminished group was that they would make for the American zone in Germany, where they might be able to talk their way into something better.

With their few months of travelling already, particularly while at the hands of the Russians, they were probably by now in Poland, but Michael wasn't clear and I can't be sure. It was summertime, so travelling was not too unpleasant. They rested in a forest during the day and walked at night. There was some hope. Farmers would give them some supplies along the way — 'bread, milk, hot water' — so they could eat and wash. One farmer in particular was very good to them, fed them well, and told his daughter to show them the way to the train station. Michael was able to buy tickets for the three of them 'and still we have some [money] left'.

Their luck had turned. They were determined to keep moving west because of their fear of the Russians — 'they never trust you, you know. You can be in big trouble.' Of course, Michael was sad that he was turning his back on his home and his family, 'but the situation was so bad, nobody want to go home then'. He would write to his mother and his family once he was settled, but he thought that, at this time, it was simply too dangerous to even think of going back home. The Russians had really put the fear of God into Michael and his mates. Yet, with increasing order coming into this confusing world and things settling down after the confusion of the last months of fighting and the first months of peace, there was some prospect for them, finally, and some little confidence for the future.

The group was lucky to find sympathetic American officers who were beginning to develop an understanding of the problem of all these homeless, stateless people. The treatment of these people was a first-order issue, along with the establishment of governance in defeated Germany, the rebuilding of all the destroyed German cities and towns, and the re-creation of the German economy. The United Nations had, in theory, taken control of all the homeless people, now to be called 'displaced persons', through the United Nations Relief and Rehabilitation Administration (UNRRA), which was largely dominated by the Americans, but represented 44 of the world's nations.

The first task for UNRRA was to open and manage orderly camps where these people might be placed, and then to feed them, settle them down, find some of them at least some type of work, and perhaps, in time, move them on to countries that might welcome them into the fold. For Michael and his group, UNRRA was an American undertaking, and they now felt secure in American hands. Europe had many vast problems and, in their minds, represented the past, with wars, fighting, poverty, and insecurity. America represented the future.

The Americans simply took control. They placed Michael and his mates on a truck and had them driven to Pilsen (now Plzen), south-west of Prague and close to the German border. From there, Michael and his mates and a large number of other people were placed on trains and taken to a displaced-persons camp in the American zone, at Aschaffenburg, near Frankfurt. There were four camps around the town, housing, Michael told me, about 20,000 people, all up. This would be Michael's home for the next four years.

Aschaffenburg (1)

SEEKING TO KNOW MORE about Aschaffenburg, I came across a short but tightly written book, *The Wild Place*, the work of an American author, Kathryn Hulme. Hulme starts her book with a dramatic flourish:

> They carried identity cards that designated them as belonging to no known country or continent but simply to a point on the compass. OST [east] ... There were some seven million of these compass-point citizens in Nazi Germany, working as slave laborers in the plane and ball-bearing factories, in the textile mills and mines, in the sugar beet and cabbage fields ... When this vast population of slaves was uncovered by the Allied armies in 1945, they had been OST people for nearly six years ... the Allies invented a new name for the OST people, indicating their state of being rather than a generalized place of origin. They were named Displaced Persons.

Her book, Hulme wrote, was about 'the slow stumbling progress of a world learning to become its brother's keeper'. While *The Wild Place* is a fine book, Kathryn Hulme is much better known for the book she wrote next.

The Nun's Story is one of the first movies I clearly remember, even to this day, though I was only a child when I saw it. I have a strong visual remembrance, still, of many of its most powerful scenes. Starring the incomparable Audrey Hepburn and the Australian Peter Finch, and based on Hulme's novel of the same name, the film tells the story of a nun, Sister Luke, trained in her native Belgium, but sent to nurse in the Belgian Congo before the war. Religious doubt and strong attraction to the doctor (Finch) finish Sister Luke's commitment to the religious life, and she petitions the Vatican for release from her vows, a highly unusual proceeding even in 1959 when the film was released.

The novel is somewhat different. While Sister Luke works closely with the (Italian) doctor in the Congo, she is sent back to Belgium, where she develops such an overpowering hatred for the German invaders that she realises that this is not compatible with religious faith and life. So she petitions to leave the convent, another European whose life was dramatically altered by war. People falsely assumed that the novelist was writing somewhat autobiographically. She was not; it was more complicated than that.

Born in 1900, and raised and educated in San Francisco, Kathryn Hulme from her early years aspired to be a writer. But war intervened and, with an intense desire to do something to help the war effort, she found herself working as a welder in an American shipyard. It was vital war work, of that there was no doubt. She doesn't tell us what impelled her towards UNRRA, but, even before the war ended, she joined the agency, where she worked from 1945 to 1951. But the ambition to be a writer still burned bright, and, returning home after her time in Europe, Hulme realised she had a story to put down on paper. The story, that is, of UNRRA and the displaced persons.

Her book, *The Wild Place*, was first published in 1953, and won the *Atlantic Monthly* Non-Fiction Award for that year. In it, she tells of her time as commandant of the UNRRA camps at Aschaffenburg, where Michael Stawyskyj was housed. *The Nun's Story* followed in 1956, based on the story of a former Belgian nun who was also working for UNRRA: '[she] told me her story through bits and parts through the long winter nights in Germany'. Hulme turned those long nocturnal conversations into a novel that swept the world; the film became its studio's highest-grossing movie ever at the time of its release.

Kathryn Hulme had not been at Aschaffenburg from the beginning; she was assigned there in 1947. 'This is where you're going', her boss said to her.

> His finger stopped at Aschaffenburg on the River Main. I remembered the town ... I saw the wide highway dropping down into it from the low Spessart Mountains, the five Wehrmacht caserns [a casern is a military barrack in a garrison town] gray and pocked from machine-gun fire, on the outskirts where the hard-core DPs [displaced persons] lived, and the shelled city at the foot of the highway where the bend in the river gleamed behind bombed red walls of an early seventeenth-century castle ...

'I'm putting you in charge', her boss said. 'Ukrainians and Estonians mainly.' She arrived two days later to discover that she had thousands of displaced persons 'of five nationalities scattered through seven camps, two of which were down the river miles away from the town.' In her first week, among many other things, she learned that 'the Ukrainians, proud, arrogant and extremely intelligent, could cry just as easily as the Poles ... when they talked about their Ukraine and its golden oceans of wheat under a wide blue sky, like their two-barred flag of blue and yellow which always had to fly blue stripe uppermost, the sky above the wheat.'

Michael had been wrong. He remembered only four camps in Aschaffenburg, but it was an easy mistake to make. There were, in fact, five in the town, but one of them housed Polish people, largely, while the remainder housed Ukrainians and Estonians, and Michael might have been thinking only of that with which he was familiar.

Then again, this is a little hard to understand, because Anna, who would soon become his wife, lived in the Polish camp, although, as a Ukrainian speaker, she preferred to spend as much time as she could with Ukrainian friends in their camps. Michael was also wrong about the number of displaced persons at Aschaffenburg. He thought there were some 20,000 people housed there, but Kathryn Hulme wrote of 9,000. Anyhow, they were very large camps.

Because each of the camps was a former military barracks, each was well built and substantial. There were three-storey brick or stone buildings of the original barracks with some wooden temporary buildings added to each site as the number of occupants threatened to swamp the accommodation. You would think there would have been a common dining room or mess hall for all the people of a particular camp, but this proved impractical. Instead, large kitchens churned out meals, which inhabitants would collect from the kitchen in an orderly fashion before returning to their own rooms to eat their meal. So you had a room of your own, I asked. 'Oh, yes', Michael replied with perhaps just a hint of pride. But not everyone had a room of their own; there were many people in dormitories. 'The food was alright', he reported, which really tells us not much at all. Soups and stews, you would imagine, and plenty of bread baked in the camp ovens. Food prepared and cooked by employed inmates, so food most likely to be to the taste of the Ukrainian people to whom it was offered. But month after month, year after year, wouldn't you have liked to have done just a bit of your own cooking?

Everything in the camps depended on the United Nations. The organisation of the camp (in general terms), the provision of food and clothing, the operation of all the facilities. But much was also devolved to the inmates. The preparation and cooking of the food, the day-to-day organisation of the camp with all manner and types of activities, sporting, cultural, and what-have-you, and the operation of the police force that any large gathering of humans would require. The displaced-persons police unit was large, and could be aggressive. Violence among the camp population could break out easily, and marital disharmony was not uncommon. Boredom will inevitably produce trouble. Boredom and the frustration of waiting. For all these people were waiting. Waiting for news.

We know that Michael and Anna married in Aschaffenburg, first in a church service and later in a civil ceremony. Sadly, Anna remains a shadowy presence in this book, though, not, of course in her children's memories and in the memories of her extended family. Michael shared little about her life before the war. You could ask him: Did she come from a big family? 'I think she had a brother and a sister.' How long had she been working in Germany? 'Oh, five years … she was only 15 or 16 when they took her away … very small girl, you know.' Like Michael, she had been to school in her village when younger, but, like Michael, she could not speak English when they left Aschaffenburg.

When I knew him, Michael didn't talk much about Anna, or life in the camp, either, for that matter. Neither the time when he first arrived nor later on when he had a wife and a small son. The stories from the years of slavery figured much larger in his mind, with their characters, their excitements, and the nature of the work that he was doing. There may be two reasons for this. Firstly, the life of a displaced person was terribly boring — monotonous, tedious, are there words to describe these years?

Secondly and more importantly, Michael had friends already in camp and he must have made new friends. He found a wife and possibly retreated into the newness of his marriage. He fathered a son, Jaroslaw, born on 17 January 1947. Becoming a new father was far from unusual at Aschaffenburg, and the joy and delight of fatherhood may well have been for Michael, again, a private, intimate pleasure.

For all his storytelling, Michael was essentially a shy and reserved man, reluctant, even with those he loved, to speak of his emotions or the deepest experiences of his life. He never said how much he missed his own family after being taken from home; he never spoke of homesickness, of loneliness, of terror. Nor did he ever speak of his love for Caterina or, later, for Anna.

Life in the camp at Aschaffenburg changed Michael forever. He became a husband and a father. But he never spoke about these changes. For him and Anna, life in the camp was about waiting. Waiting, if you like, for life to begin. To really begin. With a home somewhere in some part of the world, with work, with a growing family, please God, to feed, to educate, to love. They must have experienced great pleasure and deep joy at Aschaffenburg, but it was overlaid with boredom, with plans for the future that might be so much pie in the sky, with, every day, waiting and waiting.

Anna

HISTORIANS RARELY WRITE ABOUT people they know personally. Instead, they usually gain knowledge of those they write about through the subject's letters and diaries, the books they may have written, interviews they may have given, and through other people's opinions of the subject. I never met Charles Bean — he died in 1968 — but I have read a great deal of what he wrote, both published and his more intimate diaries; I talked at length with his wife, Effie, towards the end of her life; I spoke as well with his First World War batman, and lifelong assistant, Arthur Bazley; and I have spoken to many historians who have also written about him. So, in summary, and possibly in arrogance, I think I know the 'official' Charles Bean rather well. Though, when people ask, 'Do you think you would have liked him?', I am rather stumped.

So why should I hesitate to write about Michael's wife, my mother-in-law, Anna? It is a regret to me that I never met Anna, and perhaps therefore I feel that I can't give a rounded picture of her. But that is simplistic. Historians, as I've said, don't usually know those they write about.

Anna left few personal records, and what we have in the family papers relating to her are mostly official papers from Germany and Australia. Perhaps we can tease out a story from those forbidding official records. Among them I discovered a school report that she had deliberately preserved. I was nearly in tears when I understood its significance and what it told me about the schoolgirl who was so proud of her work and her achievement. Later, you will see the determination that both Anna and Michael brought to the schooling of their own children. This one document can explain why. As a historian, I have experienced magical and exciting moments in archives and libraries; they are moments of insight and human understanding. Opening her school report, I thought that I was close to my mother-in-law for the first time in my life. It was a revelatory moment.

Naturally, Anna left a warm place in her children's hearts and was much loved by her brother-in-law John and her sister-in-law Gina. She was intensely interested in other people, very sociable, very generous, as everyone who knew her best told me. Some have a few reservations because Anna was forthright, incredibly strong-willed, and a figure of considerable personal force. In my recollection, Michael seemed to have been slightly in awe of her. In Anna's household, no one ever must go hungry. A casual visitor would find the food piled up and the drink replenished. 'Have you had something to eat?' was the first question to anyone who walked into the house.

It's not hard to understand why she seemed such a force of nature, though she was a quite small woman. Anna was born in what was described in all the official documents as 'Seretec, Bezirk Zboricv', a place that I can't find on a map. It is somewhere in the region of Lviv, in Ukraine. She was born on 26 May 1926, and was therefore 13 years of age when war broke out. She became a zivilarbeiter in Germany, one of the seven million slaves, no later than 4 August 1942, when she was 16.

But she might have gone into slavery at an even younger age, for the August 1942 date is from an employer who retained her in service until 12 April 1945 and wrote a reference for her on 27 December 1946. The fact that she kept in touch with the family after liberation seems to confirm her own family's story that Anna was a much loved member of the household where she worked and was treated as almost a part of the family. But it is certainly possible, almost probable, that Anna worked elsewhere in Germany before entering Josef Reffel's service in Miltenberg, about 40 kilometres from Aschaffenburg. She might have been taken from her home to Germany when she was as young as 14. She would have needed great inner strength and resilience to have survived that separation at such a young age. In any case, it's certain that Anna worked as a housemaid to Josef Reffel and his family, relatively well-off Germans, who confirmed that she was a very good worker and was well liked.

Her parents, we assume, were peasant farmers like Michael's parents. Her surname was Grad, and her parents named her Paroscevia, but she gave her name on her arbeitskarte — her most official document in Germany, akin to a passport — as Paranka, a short step, perhaps, to the easier, simpler Anna. We know that she went to school, almost certainly her village school. One of her teachers made such an impression on her that, when Anna named her second child and only daughter, she used the name of the teacher, Michalina.

The school report already mentioned is dated 21 June 1937, when Anna was just 11. Almost every entry simply states that Anna had achieved a 'dobry' ('good') grade, though once or twice 'satisfactory' appears. There's no grading against prose, geography, or history, so perhaps these were not then subjects studied by 11-year-olds (or girls?). Anna missed just nine days of schooling according to her report, so she was very regular in her attendance across the 1936–1937 school year. The report is quite formal, a mixture of printing and handwriting, and it forces us to ask how it survived. It is, after all, a slight and seemingly unimportant document of a child.

Did Anna have the foresight and self-possession to take it with her from home when she was conscripted by the Germans, to prove to her future masters that she had some schooling and could be placed in better employment positions? In that sense, it was an assertion of her determination for the future. But why did she then take it into the displaced-persons camp with her? Simply because it was among her things, or again to show that she had some learning? That she was not an ignorant peasant with few prospects for a pleasing future? Then it comes all the way with her to her new home in Australia. Can we see in the improbable survival of this simple document a statement of Anna's conviction, drummed into each of her children, that education was supremely important and a passport to a better future? The school report is a simple document, perhaps, but one that speaks across the years of a tough, determined, possibly ambitious person asserting that she had some education of which she was proud.

No doubt young Anna helped her mother around the house from an early age, as she would later expect her daughter to do, and no doubt, too, there were other siblings. I would like to have known the circumstances of Anna's departure for Germany, but there is no record. Did she, like Michael, volunteer to go to Germany because the family was required to surrender one of its own or did she have no say in the matter? At such a young age, she must have missed her own family dreadfully when she left her home; she must have suffered deeply from homesickness and loneliness during her years as a slave.

Anna was indeed lucky to be working in Miltenberg, situated on the River Main, not too far from Frankfurt. This was a prosperous region of Germany, liberated quite early from Nazi control and immediately passed into American control. When and how she made her way to Aschaffenburg is not now known, but it was apparently with the acquiescence and support of the family for whom she worked, because, as I've mentioned, they kept in contact with her.

Michael says that Anna was placed in the Polish camp at Aschaffenburg, and that makes sense as she was perceived to be Polish. But she spent much of her initial time as a displaced person at the Ukrainian camp that housed Michael. She spoke Ukrainian, she believed herself to be Ukrainian, and so she preferred to be with her own people. In 1945, when she moved into the camp at Aschaffenburg, Anna was 19 years of age. How she met Michael isn't known, but he was an attractive man of 23 in 1945, with a good and strong singing voice, and he was perceived to be something of a leader among the young Ukrainians in the camp who were seeking a better life. Anna was an attractive girl: somewhat short, but with blonde hair and blue eyes, and a very lively sense of fun and good humour.

It's doubtful that Michael told Anna about Caterina, his first love. Why would he? Anna was something of a catch — practical, hard-working, attractive, and good fun. Even so, Michael must have been haunted, to an extent, by Caterina's pledge to remain true to him for however long it would take for them to be reunited. Michael would have reasoned that he needed to get on with his life, now that he was in the control of the Americans, and might have regarded a reunion with Caterina as highly improbable if not a complete fantasy. Caterina would almost certainly have remained within the Russian empire, forever unable to travel or even to move about freely.

Anna and Michael were married by the church in Aschaffenburg on 25 October 1946, when Anna was 20 years of age and Michael was 24. The document is titled 'Testimonium Copulationis' and is written entirely in Latin. Anna would have known that she was pregnant when she and Michael married, but these were people whose lives were in permanent upheaval and disjunction. Perhaps they were fortunate to be able to secure a marriage in the church at all. I wonder if, indeed, there were regular church services in the camps. (If they worried about the state recognition of religion, perhaps that is why Michael and Anna were later married again in a civil ceremony.)

Jaroslaw was born less than three months after the church wedding, with Anna still 20 years of age. I can't say whether the labour was long and difficult or if the baby had an easy birth. I can't even say who attended Anna or whether the birth was in a hospital. Given the size of the camps, and the illnesses and diseases from which the displaced persons suffered, medical services were a very high priority for the authorities, within the limits of the possible. So it's likely that Anna was well-cared for in her labour. Babies were commonplace at Aschaffenburg.

Anna was insistent that her son not be circumcised; indeed, she was adamant that this should not happen to her little baby. Her determination on this point gives some idea of the horror with which she had lived through her years of work in Germany. If Jaroslaw were circumcised, Anna reasoned, then in some future conflict, in some future age, some person in authority might consider that Jaroslaw was Jewish, and that might put his life at extreme risk.

This fragment of family remembrance, Anna's insistence that Jaroslaw not be circumcised, tells us how supremely fearful, deep down, Anna was of the world and of the men who ruled it. Life, she seemed to be indicating, was unpredictable, dangerous, and threatening. Even a little baby as beautiful as her own, with blond hair and blue eyes, the same as her own, must be protected from the evil of the world. He must never be put at risk — everything must be done to prevent him from standing out as different in this dangerous, difficult life. So this young girl was fiercely protective of her son, even in the first minutes of his life. From the first minutes, too, this boy must have begun to understand the depth of his mother's love. His parents wrapped him in love and doted on him, as new parents everywhere would want to do, but with a real sense that terror might strike at any time.

Aschaffenburg (2)

ALL THE INMATES WERE in the same boat. This was a holding camp, and every day the same questions came up: Where would they go next? Which of the United Nations countries would accept them as immigrants, and when? How slowly did the system, if it was a system, work? There was reason for some hope, because the United Nations had committed to resettling these people, but the nations worked so slowly.

Kathryn Hulme reports that each of the major accepting nations — Belgium, Canada, Britain, France, Australia, the United States, and Argentina — set up offices in one of the camps at Aschaffenburg to assess potential immigrants. Each of the nations operated somewhat differently. Australia, for example, had a preference for 'common labourers' and also had a preference for married couples with up to three unmarried children. On the other hand, Australia ignored the claims of young people with even a small number of elderly dependants. Belgium looked for single coalminers; Britain and the Netherlands looked for textile workers.

No country was interested in older people, who were likely to become a burden before they had contributed much to their new homeland. Kathryn Hulme tells the sad story of the arrival of a Belgian mission at Aschaffenburg eager to recruit single men willing to work in Belgian coalmines. There was a meeting in a camp hall, and the mission even played tape recordings of Polish immigrants happily describing the work and living conditions in Belgium. There was excitement and joy among the fit single men, as it seemed they might soon be on the move. There was also excitement generally in the camps, movement at last, some indication that the nations were beginning to make the offers that might house them all. The available places for Belgium were quickly taken up, army trucks procured for the transfer of the displaced persons to the railway, and priests recruited to bless the voyagers on their departure. Large numbers of camp inmates got up early to see off the lucky ones and wish them safe journey and good luck. This was the first substantial movement of people from Aschaffenburg, and it was quite an event. All went smoothly, and Hulme noticed the gleam in the eyes and the spring in the steps of the departing men. Resettlement was everyone's dream.

> The bright moving morning of our first emigration transport ended on a note unexpectedly forlorn and solitary. An elderly bachelor who had risen early with his roommates, as if to join in the departure watchers, walked off into the nearby woods and hanged himself ... The man had dressed neatly and completely for his final departure and had put all his essential papers in one coat pocket, as if to spare us the trouble of guesswork ... Ukrainian, male, born 1882 in Kiev, agronomist by profession and without kith or kin ...

Despair, Kathryn Hulme reported: an acknowledgement that no country was looking for old men, or amputees, for that matter, or the otherwise disabled. This despair would reappear, she noted, at random times, but mostly when there was good news for others.

It's hard to believe that Michael was ever idle, and it would seem at first that he found some work within his camp at Aschaffenburg itself, working for UNRRA almost from the time he arrived there. But he was looking for something more substantial and perhaps better paying. People were free to come and go from the camp, and, presumably as activity picked up in the region after the devastation of war, more opportunities opened up. The Americans could see that they would be in Germany for a long time (the American army remained in Aschaffenburg until 1992) and began to build permanent barracks for their troops. Michael asked for work from the Americans and they took him on.

There was always a twinkle in his eye when he told this story. He was among a group of Ukrainian boys asking the Americans for work, any kind of work. 'OK,' someone said, 'but we'll need one of you to be in charge if you're a labour force, one of you to give the orders.' They all said that Michael was their leader. 'OK,' said the American, 'form them up.' Michael had never given an order in his life, but had seen others do it — Germans, of course, many times over. So he yelled at his mates to form two straight lines, and, to his great amazement, they did it! Then he yelled at them to 'Right turn', and they did this, too; then 'March off', he barked, and they did just that. He didn't know whether to fall on the ground laughing or to swell with pride at their discipline.

Michael worked with the Americans for three years, so he must have been a good worker, and they paid in German marks: 'but nobody was caring much about money, only to get a little bit better food and something to do'. In fact, the Americans were remarkably generous with food, telling Michael to go to the cookhouse door at the end of each shift to see what might be left over from the soldiers' meals. Usually, Michael would come away with something for himself and Anna, and perhaps even for his mates. The Americans also gave their labourers cigarettes — sometimes paid them for extra work in cigarettes — and these were high currency. So now there was something to do and a little bit extra to eat and even to drink. But they were still waiting for an outcome; this was still just marking time.

Talking it over together, it was clear that, if Anna and Michael wanted to go to America, the wait would be longer. Ukrainians had already set out for America in numbers in the earlier years of the 20th century, and there were sizeable Ukrainian communities in both the United States and in Canada. Many of the Ukrainians in Aschaffenburg had given the United States as their number-one preference, or Canada, and some of them — who knew how many — had relatives, broadly construed, in those countries, and thus would be given preference by the authorities, who were keen to reunite families and develop stability.

Michael and Anna had no relatives in either country, and knew no one there. Was it worthwhile waiting on and on? Michael had a good friend, from the Sudetenland years, 'an older man than me and he was already in Tasmania for one year'. The friend wrote asking Michael to come and join him in Tasmania, and here was something positive, something that might open things up. 'But people been talking how bad is in the bush in Australia — snakes, spiders, and things like that.' And this needed to be considered, too. Was Australia simply too remote and perhaps too dangerous for these innocents from Ukraine? Michael freely admitted that he had little idea of Australia at all, but here was an invitation, something concrete, to find a new life in Tasmania and therefore some prospect of moving on from Aschaffenburg. So he and Anna put their names down for Australia and began to hope. And all those spiders and snakes? 'When they send me to Sydney, I said, "I won't move away from here."'

On his application form for Australia, Michael claimed that he had a cousin living in Western Australia. This makes little sense unless his friend in Tasmania first lived in Western Australia, which Michalina thinks was the case. But it's a mark of the desperation of displaced persons and their determination to quit the camps that applicants might have imagined distant relatives who could add stature to their application.

Finally, and it must have been in early 1949, news came through that Anna, Michael, and Jaroslaw had been accepted by Australia, and would be leaving Aschaffenburg for good within months. You would expect an outburst of joy, but Michael said he 'was not glad, because I did not know where I go, and what will be like ... was nothing much told, you know. But you just go and hope for the best.' There wasn't a big recruiting drive for Australia, or pamphlets emphasising the positives: the sun, the laid-back lifestyle, the opportunities. You simply put your name for Australia and hoped for the best. He and Anna and Jaroslaw were crossing the world, leaving all that they knew behind them, and their journey was based almost solely on hope and faith, with almost no knowledge at all to back it up. And they knew only one person in Australia, Michael's friend in Tasmania.

This really was the defining moment in their lives. But you couldn't go on at Aschaffenburg indefinitely, and you couldn't go back home. What Hitler had started in 1939 was now coming to completion. No one had foreseen this when Michael left Banyca almost ten years ago. His swift act of love and generosity had led, inexorably, to this.

Michael wrote to his mother to tell her the news, but Anna didn't write to her people. These were the early years of the Cold War, with the Russians increasingly erratic. '[Anna] didn't write home, because she was scared because her brother has some problems with Soviet government before, so when they find out if somebody overseas, oh, and they are no good people, so people being scared to write ... I write because [my people] been in Poland.'

How sad to be leaving Europe without any hope, realistically, of returning for at least a very long time, and without even a farewell message to your mother and the rest of your family. Not a word to say where you were and where you were going. But Michael wrote home to say goodbye, to write with hope for the future, to wish everyone good luck. And to turn his back on Europe with its wars and hatreds;

to strike out for something new, maybe something peaceful and prosperous. With little joy, perhaps, in departure, but with a strong hope for a better life.

Australia on the Brink

JOSEPH BENEDICT (BEN) CHIFLEY became prime minister of Australia on 13 July 1945, elected by his Australian Labor Party colleagues after the death of John Curtin, brilliant wartime leader, on 5 July 1945. Chifley had served throughout the years of the Curtin Labor government as treasurer and had performed brilliantly. Australia came out of the Second World War with no significant debt, having paid its way through the war. This put the nation in a strong place for growth and progress in the years ahead. But there remained deep challenges.

Post-war planners in the Curtin and Chifley governments realised that Australia needed an urgent, solid, and sustained boost to the population. At just seven million people, Australia didn't have a big enough workforce or capacity for growth that the post-war world would require. Natural increase, long delayed during the war years, would account for some of the necessary population growth, but migration would have to be expanded to bring in urgently needed workers. The government accepted this advice, recognising that Britain could no longer be seen as the sole, or even principal, source of migrants. The minister for immigration, Arthur Calwell, understood that Australia must play its part in helping to settle the displaced persons of Europe, but the social implications required for a significant change in the composition of the Australian people would require careful handling. Australia stood on the brink of a social revolution.

The government also needed to handle, with great sensitivity, the economic crisis the country faced. With a million men and women in uniform during the war years, the Australian economy had languished in neglect. The nation's housing stock had deteriorated badly, and there were too few houses for the returning servicemen and women, even before planners began to consider the needs of the new immigrants. An Australia-wide survey of housing needs, published in September 1944, revealed a shortage of 257,521 houses, comprising an 'actual shortage' of 175,490 homes with an additional 82,031 homes required to replace structures that were 'unfit for human habitation'. People might buy blocks of land, as my father did in East Brighton, only to spend years of frustration in trying to source builders and building supplies. Eventually, my father gave up, as others must have done, unable to see a time when he might be able to start building, and instead settled for an older and less modern home. The housing crisis meant doubling up, sharing with in-laws, or living, as we did briefly — but, for small boys, gloriously — in a hotel. Others were forced to live in areas unashamedly called 'slums'. The crisis continued well into the 1950s. Yet the housing crisis greatly stimulated the economy and ensured full employment at a time when all Australians considered this almost a part of the natural order.

The Chifley government had also to turn to the question of rationing. John Curtin, with his 'austerity drive' of 1942, had used rationing as a means of forcing the people to limit consumption so they could turn over the consequent savings to the war effort. Through enormous war-loan drives from 1942 onwards, Australians paid for the war as they went, spending much less on food and clothing while placing their savings in the war loans. But rationing was irksome, and people wanted relief from the dreariness of wartime austerity. After the war, though, Britain was in a parlous state, with heavy debt, blitzed cities, and an agricultural industry that had virtually come to a standstill. With a residual affection for Britain, Australians were prepared to allow some measure of rationing to continue if it meant the foodstuffs could be diverted to the people at 'Home'. There would be a limit, however, to the extent and duration of this generous response. Petrol rationing also continued as a drag on national life and enjoyment, and as a significant drag on the economy. Chifley maintained this rationing both because of a fuel shortage and as a further means of assisting Britain. Understandably, the people were chafing under the resulting constraints.

Nor had the peace of August 1945 heralded a new era of world harmony, as the starry-eyed might have expected. Indeed, more rapidly than was imaginable even in the last years of the war, the world entered the period of the Cold War, with the communist bloc facing off against the peoples of the western alliance. Australians entered this Cold War period anxious for world peace, but understanding the dangers the world faced. Would there be war again soon, with Russia, they wondered, although, initially, the fact that the Americans — and the Americans alone — possessed the mightiest weapon the world had ever known allowed some to downplay fears of war. When the Russians quickly caught up in the nuclear arms race, terror and anxiety increased dramatically. Australians would live through the 1950s and into the 1960s with a fear of communism as a significant element of their daily lives; a fear of armed invasion from Asia, as had seemed possible in 1942, was never far from the surface of their thinking.

Ben Chifley went into the 1946 federal election protecting John Curtin's landslide victory of 1943. There were strains and pressures on his government: Australia was a rationed, restricted, and still somewhat-dreary place, and there was fear in the air. R.G. Menzies, the failed wartime leader, was back as leader of the opposition, and tried hard to be heard speaking for the 'forgotten people'— Australia's middle class. Although Labor lost seven seats in the 1946 election, Chifley won a resounding endorsement from the voters, with

Labor holding 43 seats in the House of Representatives to 26 for Menzies' new Liberal Party of Australia. Labor would govern without interruption or disruption for the next three years.

It was a different matter at the 1949 federal election. The restrictions still irked the people, particularly the continuing petrol rationing. Menzies promised to abolish it. Fear of communism abroad and at home had grown greatly, with the prime minister forced to tackle communist militants on the New South Wales coalfields and elsewhere. Out of deep frustration with the actions of communist unions, he resorted to the use of the army to keep the coalmines open and to keep Australia warm and working throughout a bleak winter. To compound his problems in the forthcoming election, Chifley determined that the time was right to nationalise the banks in Australia. Apart from the government-owned Commonwealth Bank, Australia's banks were privately owned and deeply conservative in their policies and operations. Chifley had formed the view that the private banks were restricting the economic growth and future of Australia, and that it would be better if the government alone had its hands on the levers. With active campaigning from bank staff to their customers, turning every bank branch into something of a resource centre for Menzies' Liberal opposition, Ben Chifley had made a mighty miscalculation. In 1949, Australia stood on the brink of a significant Menzies electoral victory that would see Labor kept out of federal office for the next 23 years.

Through good luck, good management, and, it must be said, the strong and powerful economy Menzies inherited from the Curtin-Chifley years, Australia was also on the brink of long years of economic growth, of full employment, of strong population growth, and of a society altered in so many ways under the influence of an immigration program that would eventually bring in people from every part of the world. Nineteen forty-nine was a good time to be arriving in Australia for any settlers who were prepared to work hard, act prudently, and live simply. Commentators have fashionably decried the Menzies years as dull and unadventurous, and perhaps they were. But they were also years of safety and security in Australia, with an emphasis on the development of family life and modest prosperity, and on the absence of the hatreds and ideologies of earlier ages.

Paradoxically, Robert Menzies took great advantage of the Australian fear of communism. In his first years in office, he sought to outlaw the Communist Party of Australia, first by legislation and then by referendum. He failed both times, but succeeded in convincing the electorate that the communists were an omnipresent threat. Otherwise, though, he presided over a placid and unperturbed population, who enjoyed, at last, houses of adequate comfort, high car-ownership levels, and increased opportunity for all.

Wooster Victory

MICHAEL'S STORIES OF TRAVELLING to Australia focus heavily on his family. Anna, poor soul, was sick for almost the entire length of the voyage. She was not a good traveller, later prone to carsickness even on short journeys. But there was another reason for her illness on this voyage: she was carrying her second child, Michalina, who would be born in Australia, in February 1950. Michael did what he could for her, but, as the men and women on the ship were segregated into separate cabins, there wasn't a lot he could do. Though he visited her bunk bed during the day, Anna was on her own, with Joe, during the nights.

Michael would take Jaroslaw (forever after called Joe as an Australian, though often Slavko to his parents) during the day to spare Anna all the work and worry. The ship's captain made a joke that '[Joe] walks better on the deck than I do.' Joe, now two years and four months of age, was an expert little walker when the ship sailed, lively and talkative. Too good a walker, perhaps. He disappeared on one occasion, and Michael was at first seriously worried, then alarmed, and finally terrified. Joe simply couldn't be found, even though the whole ship had been turned upside down searching for him. Had he, unthinkably, fallen overboard? Simply wandered off by himself, slipped, and fallen? These were awful thoughts and real terror for Michael and Anna and the friends they had made on the ship, because children did die on these voyages. And then, at last, Joe was found, sleeping peacefully under his mother's bunk, completely unaware of all the trouble he had caused. There were tears and heartfelt thanks all round.

When Michael and Anna first looked at their ship at the docks in Naples, they saw a substantial, sleek, newly refurbished vessel. It was called *Wooster Victory*, indicating that it was a member of the Victory class of ships, which were originally designed as troopships and built in the United States. The Victory class took over from the Liberty class, and was built from 1944 onwards. There were 97 ships in this class, with reasonably austere accommodation for troops crossing the Atlantic. Built to house 1,597 men, the ships were of a very basic design, with multi-tiered bunks installed between decks and in the cargo holds. There were numerous toilet and shower blocks throughout the ship.

Wooster Victory had only come into service in April 1945, crossing the Pacific and arriving in Melbourne in May 1945. Bought by the Sitmar Line after the war, and subsequently refitted in February 1948 to transport displaced persons, the ship could carry 900 passengers 'under conditions that, while not luxurious, were quite pleasant'. *Wooster Victory* became the sixth vessel to carry displaced persons to Australia, commencing service in this work at Genoa in August 1948.

For its third displaced-persons voyage for 1949, *Wooster Victory* left Naples on 30 June carrying 885 passengers, including Michael, Anna, and Joe. It was destined for Sydney, via Port Said, Aden, Colombo, and Fremantle. All passengers would disembark at Sydney. As a displaced-persons ship, there were, of course, no classes on board. All were housed in very big spaces, cabins of up to 300 passengers in bunk beds. All ate the same food and all were treated equally.

A passenger on *Wooster Victory*'s previous voyage, docking in Melbourne on 24 May, has left a detailed account of that voyage. There is some difference between the official record and the passenger's account of the May sailing, but the two accounts can be reconciled. Sitmar's historian, Peter Plowman, states that this voyage originated in Genoa, as with *Wooster Victory*'s earlier sailings, while the passenger writes clearly of the ship leaving Naples. I don't imagine you would forget the sight of Mount Vesuvius or your arrival at Naples after a long train journey or your two weeks in a displaced-persons camp nearby, and so the passenger's memory seems reliable and authentic. Perhaps both accounts are correct. The ship may indeed have started its voyage at Genoa and called in at Naples to pick up additional passengers.

The passenger who has left us her account was married and had two little daughters, had been in a displaced-persons camp in Germany for nearly four years, and, like Michael, Anna, and Joe, had been cleared for Australia after rigorous checks, including a medical check-up. She writes of her 'emaciated and exhausted-looking husband and me looking the same beside him' staring out from a photograph on the day of their departure from their German camp.

They were taken by train, 'in cold, unheated railcars', from Germany, across Austria, and all the way down Italy to Naples, just as Michael and Anna and Joe were a month or so later. The passenger found the city to be a shambles — 'ruined, impoverished, bedraggled' — and she was shocked to see that local children rushed the train crying out for bread, seeking help from people who had nothing to give. The passenger and her family spent a couple of weeks waiting for the arrival of their vessel at Naples and then found themselves on the wharf about to board their ship. They saw that it was called *Wooster Victory*. Once again, their papers were checked, probably for the last or second-last time, because they would soon be new residents of Australia, where asking for papers was unheard of. On board, the travellers were sent straight to the dining room, 'where a marvellous vision awaits us — on long tables stand bowls piled high with white fragrant bread, and on each individual plate a boiled egg and stalk of willow — a symbol of Easter!' The Australian consul in Naples 'greets us warmly as future citizens of his country and wishes us a Happy Easter and a safe and pleasant journey'.

Crossing the Mediterranean, most of the passengers were seasick, almost all of them at sea for the first time in their lives. They stopped briefly at Port Said, and local sellers offered all sorts of amazing things for sale. Those who bought the watermelons, bananas, and other perishables were ordered to throw them overboard when the ship departed — who knows what illnesses and other problems the fruit might have caused. As *Wooster Victory* passed through the Suez Canal, the passengers had the opportunity of seeing the desert for the first time, and the oases, the 'small humble daubed houses', and some of the locals at work. In the trying, hot conditions, several of the children aboard fell ill, and a local doctor at Aden advised the removal of those families with sick children to hospital, as the children may not have survived until the next port, Colombo.

'We have left Ceylon at last and approach the equator. The heat is unbelievable! On the deck the sailors have stretched a canvas to protect us from the sun ... in the cabins and below deck it is sheer hell.' A child died and was buried at sea, and the passenger heard 'someone's inconsolable weeping'. Her own child became ill with a kind of tropical fever, and the woman spent all night 'sponging her small feverish body with a wet cloth in order to somehow reduce her raging temperature. I tremble, I weep, I pray.' But the journey passed, and, 'after a difficult journey of 30 days we sight land on the horizon ... our *Wooster* has docked in Melbourne'.

It must have been very like this for Anna, Michael, and Joe sailing from Naples a month later. The medical records for the three of them are in the National Archives of Australia in Canberra: all were in good health, with good teeth and excellent blood pressure. There was a chest X-ray of each attached to the file to show that none suffered from tuberculosis. There's a photograph of each of the three travellers, and Joe steals the show as a very beautiful little boy.

Joe suffered no sickness during the voyage, unlike his unfortunate mother, and Michael never spoke of deaths at sea. But who knows? The tragedies would have been kept out of the sight of passengers as far as possible. It was rough at sea, but only once, and only for about 24 hours: 'big strong men were sick. Only me and Joe not sick!' Michael laughed at the memory.

The ship stopped at Fremantle for a full day on making Australian landfall, to take on more coal; 'we been glad to see any city or something like that, you know'. Then it was straight on to Sydney. 'Oh, was a beautiful sight [the harbour], but I still don't know what will happen, where I will be.' Was he excited at being in Sydney? 'No, no. You just think what will happen. What will happen now?' But happy to be on the land, anyway.

It was hard, so hard. Neither Michael nor Anna spoke any English yet, and would have been relying on an interpreter to tell them where they were going and what the immediate future would bring. What did they know of Australia, these newest Australians? Very little, in truth. That it was a very long way from Europe; that they could never see themselves making a return journey. That they had virtually no money, though both had a keen will to work. That they had no idea about the way of life of Australians, their system of government, the goodness or otherwise of the people who would be placed in authority over them. They had no idea how they might go about finding some accommodation, some work, a fair wage. Would they be placed on a farm, which was what Michael knew, or would they be placed in other work? They did know, at least, that they would be found work, to pay off the cost of their voyage and all the other costs of landing in Australia. It isn't hard to understand Michael's memory of his anxiety as he finally stepped off *Wooster Victory*.

A New Home

THE SECOND WORLD WAR had given Australians a thorough fright. For the first time ever, it looked as though the worst fears of this tiny (in population terms) British outpost on the edge of Asia might indeed experience defeat, possibly even invasion, at the hands of the Japanese. Nineteen forty-two had been a grim year, with the fall of Singapore demonstrating the folly of relying on the British in 'the Far East', the sinking of the capital ships *Repulse* and *Prince of Wales* demonstrating the power of the Japanese air force, and the Allied defeat in Malaya showing the power of the Imperial Japanese Army. For a time in 1942, Australia seemed to stand alone and defenceless against a vastly superior Japan. It would take years for Australians to recover from these shocks and batterings.

As I've mentioned, a Labor government had been in charge throughout the years of crisis and had carried Australia, nervously, into a post-war world. Arthur Calwell, a Melbourne man and future leader of the party, was immigration minister, and, as such, it was his job to encourage significant population growth while at the same time ensuring full employment for all. Australia had suffered badly during the massive economic disruption of the 1930s, and full employment was now regarded as such a settled plank of policy among the political classes that it seemed to be almost an Australian birthright. Calwell expected and planned for 2 per cent annual population growth, half of it through natural increase (the births of those who would come to be called 'the baby boomers') and half of it through immigration.

Britain, the traditional origin of Australian immigrants, could not, by itself, meet this latter target. There were still plenty of '£10 Poms', of course — though Churchill was calling on his fellow Britons not to desert their home — but the shipping simply couldn't be found for mass British migration, even if the will was there. Available shipping had instead been diverted to move the displaced persons wasting away in camps everywhere, who simply must be resettled if Europe was to have any kind of recovery and post-war economic prosperity. So while Australia had a humanitarian imperative to work with other members of the United Nations to help solve the displaced-persons problem, it had an economic and security imperative as well. Calwell had to sell an immigration program to the Australian public that looked away from Britain and towards the peoples of Europe; first to the Balts (as the blue-eyed blonds from the Baltic states were known in Australia), then to the northern Europeans (seemingly a lot like Australians, though initially lacking any understanding of English), and then — possibly, eventually — even to look to the southern Europeans (short, dark, and swarthy).

While UNRRA was establishing its camps in Germany and beginning to house the homeless millions, the United Nations also established, in April 1946, the International Refugee Organisation (IRO), of which Australia was one of the 26 founding nations. IRO's job was to resettle the displaced persons from the camps and to persuade member governments to take more and more people from these camps. With IRO funding and access to IRO shipping, Australia could play a part. A small part, though — too large a number of refugees might unsettle Australians at home.

In July 1947, Australia and IRO signed an agreement that Australia would take a minimum of 12,000 refugees a year. The arrangement was that the refugees would work for two years after their arrival at the direction of the government, to be housed in migrant camps and hostels. Thereafter, they would be free to strike out on their own. This meant that, in their first two years, when they probably spoke little or no English, they would not be thrown in among ordinary Australian workers, and that they would be no threat to the jobs of these Australian workers. In a sense, they would be segregated from the broader community, or protected from it, living among their own and largely working among their own.

It wasn't easy for Australia to suddenly find the hostels and camps that would be needed for this experiment, so Calwell turned to the former army and air-force camps that were now being decommissioned in most states. At a time of acute housing shortage in Australia, these camps could quickly be pressed into service for the 'reffos', as they soon came to be called. Calwell insisted that the migrants could not become involved in any industrial disputes that might arise in their workplaces, and, indeed, if a dispute arose in the workplace, the migrant workers would be taken back to their camps or hostels and paid unemployment benefits until the dispute was resolved. There would be no place for troublemakers among the migrants. In Australia's scheme, the new migrants had two years of guaranteed employment and accommodation, during which time it was expected that they would learn the language and customs of the country that — it was hoped — they would soon be calling their home.

The government proceeded cautiously so as not to 'scare the horses'. Australians were wary, to put it mildly, of any potential migrants except Britons, Canadians, New Zealanders, and Americans. And they weren't too sure about the Yanks, either, coming over here and making merry hell with our girls during the war. Now they were expected to open the country to all these reffos from Europe, and who knew how *they* would fit in. They didn't even speak our language, they likely knew nothing about cricket or the gee-gees, and they played an odd brand of football, quickly dubbed 'wog-ball'.

The first refugees to reach Australia, all 843 of them, under the July 1947 IRO agreement, docked at Port Melbourne in November 1947 to a carefully orchestrated arrival. They were a carefully selected bunch, comprising Latvians, Lithuanians, and Estonians — healthy, good-looking, happy people seemingly dreamed up in central casting for the newsreel cameras and the newspaper reporters. The minister had decreed that no one in the first 'choice sample' be under the age of 15 or over the age of 35, and all had to be single. There were to be no Jews among them. Calwell reported that 'the men were handsome and the women beautiful. It was not hard to sell immigration to the Australian people once the press published photographs of that group.'

The newspapers were delighted with the first arrivals. 'The migrants are healthy, handsome,' the Melbourne *Argus* reported, 'but in many young faces are the marks of separation from parents, years of hard labour in German camps.' The average age of the migrants was 24, the paper said, and they include farmers, teachers, office workers, students, waitresses, and stenographers. 'All are unmarried, but many became engaged during the trip … In spite of having no money, a minimum of luggage, and very small wardrobes, the party was uniformly cheerful and optimistic.' As Arthur Calwell left the ship after welcoming the refugees to Australia, 'groups of migrants sang folk songs in his honour'.

These people carried a heavy responsibility to convince Australians to see them as genuine and likeable settlers. On arrival, it was reported that a Commonwealth health inspector had found no evidence of tuberculosis among them. It was imperative that they be healthy. It was also necessary that they seem happy in their new surroundings. This first group was taken to a former army camp at Bonegilla (near Wodonga in north-eastern Victoria), which would soon grow into one of Australia's largest ever migrant camps. The new arrivals might have been apprehensive, or homesick, or downright scared to be out there in the Australian bush, but, for the cameras and notebooks of the reporters, they had to appear content and confident. Perhaps it was a good thing that few of them spoke English.

The IRO-Australia scheme grew quickly from these humble beginnings. By 1949, IRO had 19 ships on the Naples–Australia run, and, in that year, 75,486 displaced persons arrived in Australia, greatly exceeding the 12,000 minimum first envisaged. The scheme ceased in 1954, by which time more than 170,000 refugees had been settled in Australia. IRO itself was closed down by the United Nations to be replaced by the United Nations High Commission for Refugees (UNHCR), which still operates. Australia had accepted the refugees with the best attempt at putting on as good a face as it could muster, but it would be foolish to suggest that these 'new Australians' were universally welcomed.

Bathurst

IT WAS A FINE MILD DAY in Sydney on 31 July 1949 when *Wooster Victory* docked at just after nine o'clock in the morning. Seas were slight and there was a westerly wind, but it would be a colder night. It was a Sunday, and Sydney was asleep, as it would be all day because Australian Sundays then were a real 'day off': nothing happened. The passengers didn't disembark on arrival, but had to wait for officials to process them on the next working day, Monday. Each adult from *Wooster Victory* was given a voucher with a small money value, just so that they would have something, and there was a medical check-up to ensure that all were fit to land. Then, on Monday 1 August, it was down the gangplank and off the ship for the first time since Naples. They were now on dry land, and this may have had Anna feeling better already. There were no reporters or newsreel cameramen to greet this group; the arrival of migrants — the DPs, the reffos — was routine by now.

There were buses waiting on the docks, ready to take this new group to Central railway station for the train trip to Bathurst. Bathurst, a substantial town, 200 kilometres to the west of Sydney and across the Blue Mountains, was the site of a former army camp, the only place in New South Wales big enough to receive and house the immigrants. Though the travellers did not know it yet, they were lucky that the railways had enough coal to fuel their train to Bathurst, because, in winter 1949, Australia was in the midst of industrial turmoil. The coalmines were all but closed down, and Labor prime minister Ben Chifley already had troops stationed on the coalfields, and said he would send the troops down the mines if the miners continued their strike. This would, in fact, happen, within the next few days.

Communism was a word these refugees may have thought they had left behind in Europe. Communism and Soviet inflexibility had prevented them returning to their homes in Ukraine, Poland, Lithuania, Estonia, and elsewhere; none of the new arrivals had any reason to think well of communists. Unfortunately, communism was also a fact of life in Australia. It was a word that currently dominated the reporting in every Australian newspaper as the refugees from *Wooster Victory* landed. It was a word that would later destroy young Joe Stawyskyj's life and blight his parents' lives.

The army had moved into Bathurst in 1940 when the 1st Armoured Division of the AIF was housed there. Well, not quite in Bathurst, because it's wise not to put troops too close to a large town, and, in any case, the land would be very much more expensive closer in to town. So the army camp was placed on Limekilns Road at Kelso, about ten kilometres from Bathurst. The camp grew substantially during the war when later it was designated an infantry training centre. Built to the standards deemed good enough for soldiers at war at that time, Bathurst Army Camp had long wooden or iron huts with corrugated iron roofs, ablution blocks, mess halls, no heating in the huts, few made roads, and little attempt at beautification.

Compared to the camp at Aschaffenburg, a former German army barracks, this camp was primitive. Many of the buildings at Bathurst were in bad repair, and could not be repaired or replaced in the foreseeable future because Australia had an acute shortage of building materials — and, due to the strikes, not much more was coming down the supply line. Single people were placed in one set of huts, on narrow beds, dormitory style. Married people were in similar huts, but these were partitioned off into separate sections for each couple and any children.

The camp had been designed to hold 1,500 soldiers in the war years, but, at its closing as a migrant camp in 1952, it consisted of 11 self-contained long huts and could officially house up to 6,000 people. Initially, there was a great deal of overcrowding, and some migrants were even placed in tents, which can't have been ideal in the icy Bathurst winter. The total population at the camp was usually about 8,000 people, which tells us how crowded it was. Between 1948, when it opened, and 1952, when it closed, Bathurst held altogether over 100,000 migrants. Most of these people travelled by train from Sydney to Kelso and then by bus to the camp. In the nature of the journey, many arrived at the camp late in the evening or at night, and finding their way about on that first night must have been close to a nightmare.

Michael remembered arriving at Bathurst at night and being shown to their 'room', as he called it, though it was, in reality, a partitioned-off space in a larger hut. But at least there was some privacy, and he and Anna were able to sleep together again after the month of separation on the ship. It was very cold in Bathurst, he remembered — 'a cold night with frosts inland', the paper said — and the staff gave him some blankets 'and that's all … We have to go to the kitchen to get some food' (surely he meant the dining hall). Others would soon be complaining, 'we are sick of sausages, stew, and spinach', but Michael was happy and relieved: '[the food] was good compared with what we had before … in Germany or in Russian camp'.

This first night in a new country, which they hoped to make their permanent home, feels as though it should have been momentous for Anna and Michael. I want to hear a fanfare of trumpets, a roll of drums, I want to think of them looking up at the Australian night sky in wonderment and awe, so different from the night sky they had known in Europe. I want to hear them talking of their hopes and aspirations in this new land, for themselves and Joe and for the baby yet to be born. I wonder if they were proud to be in Australia, even here, out in the bush, and pleased to have escaped Europe and the menacing communists. But I know it wasn't like that.

There were, of course, no trumpets or drums, and, if there was talk, it was unlikely to have been grand or future focused. In all likelihood, they straightened up their room a bit and made up their beds, rejoiced in their full stomachs after the dreary hours on the train, but missed their coffee and wondered about the dark brew of tea — a part, it seemed, of every Australian meal. Anxiously, they must have settled Joe down and tried to get him off to sleep, an excited little boy in new quarters again. 'More of these blankets for Joe, keep the boy warm', and then into bed themselves, to hold each other tight for the first time for a month. Hopefully, sleep came, and peace and some contentment. The days ahead were full of the unknown, and there would be much to do. The first thing: to learn the language. There could not be much work without that.

The men emerged the next morning from their sleep expecting to be given work within a few days: this was the contract. Once in work, they would begin to earn money to buy what they needed and perhaps to save a little bit for the future. But these hopes were quickly shattered. Australia was on strike, it seemed, and they certainly could not be placed in work. If they had been given work, they would have been called scabs or strike-breakers, and the government's peaceful implementation of its agreement with IRO would collapse into hatreds and abuse. Migrants, instead of being welcomed, would be reviled, so the government had to keep them out of work and in the camp, almost hidden from sight.

It was the worst possible outcome for the newcomers. Instead of work and money in wallets and purses, the new arrivals would be confined to the camp, given unemployment benefits, and told to go on with the waiting that had been such a long part of their lives. The irony of it: men hopeful for the future, eager to work, thankful to have escaped European hatreds and communism, and now caught up in a government stand-off between bosses and communist-controlled unions. It really would make a strong man cry.

As before, Michael's good luck held. A young Ukrainian man came up to Bathurst to see these new Ukrainian arrivals, to see if there were any from his former group whom he may perhaps have known. And he had known Michael. He was a good piano player, this young man, Michael said, perhaps the life of any party going among the Ukrainians at Aschaffenburg. He was working in a Sydney hostel as an assistant manager, and he said to Michael that he could get him a job in the kitchen as a kitchen hand if he wanted it. There was no strike there — the Commonwealth was the employer, and the workers were content, and all of them were immigrants, anyway.

And this hostel? Well, it was at Meadowbank on the banks of the Parramatta River in the west of Sydney, a small hostel of only about 100 people. And his wife and Joe, could they come, too? Unfortunately not, it was a hostel for single men only, just recently built to bring workers closer to where the work was in Sydney. Anna and Joe would have to stay behind at Bathurst, at least until Anna had given birth to her new baby, possibly longer. But Michael would be in work, being paid wages for the first time in his life, with his foot on the ladder at last, even if on the lowest rung. 'I pick it [agree to it] because this boy knew me, he put me on work in a hostel, so that was my contract.'

Michael was earning, he remembered, £6 a week, which was fair money, as a kitchen man. But I wonder whether that was right. In July 1951, just a few weeks before his arrival, the basic wage in Sydney was set at £9/13/-, and surely the Commonwealth was paying its workers the basic wage? Until I remember that they would have deducted his board and lodging from his wage, so perhaps £6 was about right. And what was he doing in the kitchen at Meadowbank? 'Just wash the dishes and give out food and things like that … washing vegetables, peeling potatoes … for me was good because I was happy, I was singing like mad.' When he was happy, Michael did sing; in the mountains above his village at home, even in the fields of the farms he worked on in Sudetenland, 'they can hear me three villages [away]'. And, at Meadowbank, this caught people's attention — caught the eye of his boss, the cook, who was also Ukrainian, but an older man than Michael.

And the boss came to like Michael very much, not just for the singing, although that was, naturally, a part of it. On one occasion, one of the other workers — they were 'all mixed up', Yugoslav, Polish, Latvian — one of these workers complained to the boss that Michael, who was on sandwich duty, was going too slowly. Look, the man said, at the number of sandwiches I have made while Michael has only made one. 'Oh,' said the boss (and, in the storytelling, Michael could really draw out that 'Oh'), 'but Michael makes *very* good sandwiches.' On another occasion, the boss asked Michael to watch over the Christmas puddings he had made for the residents as a special treat. Michael thought the fire in the oven needed a bit of help, and built it up, burning all the puddings to a cinder. But the cook was not cranky or anything like that; he just laughed at Michael and started again with his second batch of puddings.

Meanwhile, Anna and Joe were at Bathurst. 'We been used to situations like that. She knew I come to see her if I can and she understood if I can't, I can't see her … You could go for weekends if you arrange it with the staff in the kitchen, but problem was we did not know from start which way to go, how to go.' Michael was, of course, just picking up English, and, as most of the residents in the hostel at Meadowbank were British, they helped him to learn. But at the start he had no English: 'How to buy a ticket, or ask for direction or anything like that … but anyhow, we went once after three or four weeks, we pick up a train in Strathfield, somehow it was right train.'

A Friday-night train, probably, because Michael arrived at Bathurst station at about three in the morning.

'Everything is dark, you did not know in which direction go to camp, so we walking around. There's one light there, we went there and knocked on the door. Policeman come out, we try to ask him where the camp is but we didn't know [the word] "camp".' It might have been pretty obvious to the policeman, I would have thought, a bunch of migrant blokes, obviously lost, very early in the morning, probably off the train from Sydney. One of them tried a bit of German, 'lager, lager you know, in German is "camp"'. Perhaps the policeman thought they were looking for a beer at that time of night. In any case, he was no help at all and seems just to have sent them on their way. Somehow, by luck, they chanced on the right road to the camp. And lucky again, the milkman came down the road with his horse and cart to deliver milk to the camp. 'Come on, hop up, so he bring us to the camp … That was first time. After was alright.'

Michael was alone at Meadowbank for nearly two years. He went to Bathurst regularly, when he could, and certainly for the birth of his second child. 'I don't know exactly when I bring them back; when I get accommodation with friends of Michalina's godmother' (a friend Anna had made in the camp). Housing was so short in Sydney, and it really was remarkable that people would be prepared to put strangers up, but they were Ukrainians and they knew that the community had to hang together. Michalina was born in February 1950 and was still a baby when they moved to Sydney, so the move was likely to have happened some time in 1950. Though Michael still needed to live at Meadowbank for his work in the hostel, the house they had found was at Sefton, in Sydney's west, a couple of train rides away, and quite a short distance as the crow flies, about 15 kilometres, so perhaps, from time to time, he walked. He did try to get there most nights for a bit of time with his family.

The money was good now 'because I was lucky enough on roster days [off] to get job with plumber there in Meadowbank. He pay me nearly for two days as much as I get for whole week in [the] kitchen.' So Michael was just about doubling his wage by working a seven-day week, but he said that the work in the kitchen wasn't hard or demanding, and he still had time to see his family most nights. Anna and the children lived at Sefton for the best part of a year, but then they had to move on. 'They moved to some Australian [man's house] ... I forgot his name now ... He give us accommodation there for six months, he said, but we stay only about four months because I bought a block of land and build a garage and we moved to garage.'

I can't tell you who this Australian man was and how it was that he offered accommodation to this Ukrainian family. The house was again in Sefton, so perhaps Michael met the man on his way to and from his visits to his family, and perhaps the man took a shine to him. A young bloke, he might have observed of Michael, one of those reffos, but hard working, friendly, and a good family man. Just the type we need in this country, not like those bloody commo agitators. If the man had taken a good liking to Michael, this would not have been unusual in Michael's life. Perhaps this Australian man also helped Michael to buy his land at Fairfield, in the western suburbs, although no doubt Michael's English was quite good by now after nearly two years among English speakers at Meadowbank. Michael had a real ear for language: he had picked up so much in his adventures so far, and now, with seven languages, he had a real advantage over many other workers.

The Fairfield land Michael bought may have been a government release in a rapidly growing Sydney, or Michael might have bought it from a private seller. I'm inclined to think it was private land, because there was just one street of it, and all the surrounding land remained paddocks for a long time (it later became an industrial estate). Michael remembered that he paid £180 for his land, £120 down and the remainder to be paid off over time (which doesn't sound like government land either).

With his remaining savings, he bought, with difficulty because of the lack of supplies, the materials with which to build his garage. Once built, the family lived in the garage for the next few years while Michael built his house. In the last seven weeks of his life, when Michael finally left the house he had built and had lived in for over 50 years, the garage was still standing, though now somewhat battered and a bit shabby. What pride and love was invested in that garage. Anna and Michael's first Australian home.

Bell Crescent

BELL CRESCENT, FAIRFIELD, is a cul-de-sac (we used to call them dead-end streets, in Australia) that runs for about 700 metres, wedged between the railway line and Prospect Creek. It takes its name from the Bell family who once (briefly) owned Cambridge House, a grand Victorian mansion close by. There is only one way into Bell Crescent, off Pine Road, and no way out, unless you turn around and go back out to Pine Road. You would only enter Bell Crescent if you were visiting folk there or if you lived there. Most of the houses on the right-hand side, the even-numbered side of the crescent, run down to Prospect Creek at their back, while almost all the houses on the left-hand side, the odd-numbered side, have the railway line at their back fence. Being such an isolated street, Bell Crescent makes for good neighbours. Many of the houses have recently been rebuilt, or soon will be, in common with so many other suburban properties in the older suburbs, but some are still originals.

When Anna and Michael bought their land on Bell Crescent, in 1951, there were few houses in the street, possibly only two. The road was unmade, and the street, like most of the suburb of Fairfield, was not sewered (these defects were not remedied until the 1970s). You could buy land in Fairfield then for under £100 ('level block, conv stn schools'), so, at £180, Michael and Anna had gone for something a little bit better. Perhaps the dead-end nature of the street appealed — safer for a little boy and a little girl, who most likely would soon be playing with other little boys and girls out in the street. You could get a good game of footy going, or a rousing version of cowboys and Indians, without the constant interruption of cars coming down the street. Or perhaps it was the size of the block that was attractive, because it was a big block, with plenty of room, later, for chooks and a vegetable garden. Few of the residents would have had cars in the early days in any case, so a car in the street was a bit of a novelty. Most people walked the short distance to the Fairfield shops, or to the station if going further afield.

I don't know if someone had recommended Bell Crescent to Michael and Anna before they bought their land, but, given the nature of the settlement there, it would seem likely. This was deeply migrant territory, even displaced-persons territory. The Hanleys had a small corner shop at the beginning of Bell Crescent, though it was really on Pine Road. Then, at numbers two and four, were Australian families (the Whites and the Youngs); then followed at number six a Czech family, then a Polish family; at number 12, there was a Russian family, the Lyschnkos, who put up the first brick house in the street; then there was a Russian/Ukrainian family, Simon and Zena, at number 14; Michael, Anna, Joe, and Michalina were at number 16, followed by a Polish family, an Australian family ('Aunty Tops and Uncle Dave'), another Australian family, a German family, and then Czechs, though they had no children. Coming back up to Pine Road on the other side of the street, there was a Polish/Hungarian family, Czechs, one Italian, two Aussies, an unknown, a Ukrainian family (Mrs Parachinutz), a Ukrainian/Russian family (Lala), a Hungarian family, and, finally, an Italian family. It must have been wonderful to walk down the street at dinnertime, with all the powerful competing aromas. Was the piroshky as good as the pasta or as good as the goulash? And what of the pirohi and the vareniki as compared to the schnitzel or a mixed grill?

The first thing was to build the garage, so the family could move in and Michael could stop wasting money on board, lodging, and rent. It was hard to get the building materials, but somehow Michael obtained the supplies from a builder he had met, and the builder cut the materials into the right sizes for the garage. Then 'just friends of mine come together and we put up and that's all'. There was a kitchenette right by the door of the garage, in a little entry alcove; then the quite long garage was divided into two rooms, one for living and sleeping, and one for sleeping. The garage was lined and had linoleum covering the floorboards. There were a couple of windows. There was also an outhouse with a toilet and pan (and newspaper squares for toilet paper). The family washed at a basin that could be moved around as needed, but, a couple of nights a week, Joe and Michalina would be given a bath in a tin wash tub, kept outdoors for most of the year, though it would have been brought inside in winter. Living in the garage was cosy and it was comfy, and the Stawyskyjs were not the first people on Bell Crescent to be living in a garage — the Klauses, next door at number 18, for one, certainly did this, too. And there must have been others in the street doing the same. It was a sensible and practical solution to Australia's post-war housing crisis.

Michael says he bought his land at Fairfield because it was cheaper than, say, North Ryde or Meadowbank, where he would have preferred to have lived. Land at North Ryde, he thought, cost about £300, and that was just too expensive. And, at Fairfield, he was close to the railway and, therefore, able to get to work along the western-suburbs line easily enough.

When his contract with the Commonwealth was just about finished, Michael asked for and was given a slightly early release, after not quite two years, and then he went to work for Amalgamated Wireless (Australasia) Ltd (AWA), Australia's largest and most prominent electronics company, at Ashfield. It was good work and paid well ('we used to double what wages [were] worth on a bonus'). Michael said that, whenever he asked about a possible job with any prospective employer, he always asked about overtime, to make sure he could get as much as he could for his labour. He was retrenched from AWA after about two years because the company was converting its large Ashfield factory to the production of television sets, having saturated the market with radios and radiograms, which had previously been its staple.

Michael used the downtime (measured in days, not weeks) after AWA to clean up his block, before starting to build the permanent house that he would put up. He then took a job with a builder, to learn all he could about building a house. The builder was an Austrian man, and the other workers, largely carpenters, were all Germans, so Michael felt right at home. The builder was in a great hurry to get on with his houses, so great was the need, and Michael was working 14–16 hours a day, he said. There was a lot of overtime, of course: 'work hard, very hard work because they want to work fast, you know. But was good because was lot of money.'

Michael had to make a start on his house because it certainly wouldn't build itself. It took him about three years to finish it, he remembered. 'It was good because you live on the place where you build, so early you get up, you started working. Well, that's life.' Michael had the plans drawn up by an architect, but it was quite a simple design. There were two rooms across the front of the house, with a front door and hallway in the middle. The front room on the left-hand side as you faced the house was the main bedroom; across the hallway was a similarly sized room, which was the living room; down the hallway was a bathroom and toilet on the left, and another bedroom; behind the living room on the right was another bedroom. The house then finished off with a small dining area and quite small kitchen, but all well appointed. The laundry was out in the backyard, which stretched out on its way down to the creek. The total length of the block was 270 feet (82 metres).

The house was a very solid construction, standing on brick piers; the external walls were fibro, and the window frames were wooden. The floors were wooden, and the skirting boards were particularly solid and handsome in a blond wood. There was a picture rail running around each of the rooms. It was a compact and pleasant house, looking out onto Bell Crescent confidently. Michael planted a lawn of couch grass in back and front, there were rose bushes along the front fence, and there were vegetable gardens in the back, with good soil from Prospect Creek, and good growth. There was a chook house right down the back, with maybe up to 24 hens, which Joe and Michalina looked after. There was plenty of work for everyone to do, even the little ones. But there was enough time for play and fun out on the street, too, once the chores had been done.

Michael worked with his builder mates for a couple of years and then found work at a woollen-mills factory in Marrickville, 'because it was a little bit slack with the work in this moment … was very good job. Very good job and the foreman like me and everybody [likes me] … I was oiling the spinning machines … very easy and good job.' In Europe, Michael had worked outdoors either on farms or in the forests, but, in Australia, he became a factory worker — and quite a skilled worker for that matter. 'Oh, is easy. They show you, and I was young and I pick up very quickly. When I went to AWA, they ask me about experience … did you work anywhere on machines? Oh, I said, yes, in Germany, we work with these electric bulbs, you know … They show me and straightaway I work. Was no problem at all. Been happy with it.' And if he was happy, was he singing in his factory work? Very likely. But did he miss his own home and the village he had grown up in? 'For a while, I miss the mountains. I miss mountains and I miss air, you know. Like, sometimes I still think when I was in Meadowbank and it was hot, I was thinking I was fresh and nice in summer in the mountains — I feel like I have not enough air to breathe, you know. I remember that … but you get used to it, you know.'

There was a nice house now, and a good job, and the children were in school at Our Lady of the Rosary, Fairfield, in the care of the Sisters of St Joseph. Michael had no debt and had a regular income. Was this not the good Australian life? Was this not the reason for leaving Europe and starting again in the new world? Michael was well liked by his workmates, and would even join a few of them in the Railway Hotel in Fairfield after work on Friday for a beer or two. There was talk of a Ukrainian Catholic parish in Lidcombe, which would create a stronger Ukrainian community and deepen friendships.

There was sadness for Anna and Michael when their third child, a boy, died shortly after his birth; but, years later, there would be another baby boy, John, born in 1963. Anna found work in a leather-tanning factory in Fairfield that was staffed mostly by Ukrainians, and her wages were very useful. The children did well in school, speaking Ukrainian at home but English at school. The parish school was very crowded, of course, with over 600 students crammed into the few classrooms. There were about a dozen nuns in the community at Our Lady's, a sign that religious service was still a big part of Catholic life. Later, Joe would attend Patrician Brothers' College Fairfield (opened in 1953), and Michalina would go to Cerdon College in Merrylands in the care of the Marist Sisters (opened in 1960).

We might look in on this family again in 1960 to see how things are. Michael is 38 years of age, Anna is 34, Joe is 13, and Michalina 10. Michael is now working at Crane Copper and Aluminium Pty Ltd in Concord. He started there in May 1954, as a plate shearsman, 'and has performed his duties to our entire satisfaction'. He is now responsible for training newcomers, likes the work, and is both well liked and respected by his bosses and co-workers. He's a shy man who doesn't open up easily, but his remarkable language skills make him valued at the factory, and he often translates for his co-workers. He has begun to take an interest in Australian sports like cricket and rugby league, and can talk with his co-workers about these sorts of things. But he wants something closer to home, and, in October 1962, he will take a job at Borg-Warner — makers of car and truck gearboxes — at Yennora, as a machinist.

When Michael joined Borg-Warner, Australia hadn't yet developed its long-enduring love affair with the motor car, but there was more than a glint in the eye; romance was just around the corner. Coote and Jorgensen, an Australian company, had started making car replacement parts after the war. They bought land in what was then Fairfield and built a factory complex there, before being bought by Borg-Warner, a large American corporation, in 1958. The new subsidiary made 'automotive and tractor transmissions and driving axles and their components; industrial and locomotive gearboxes, speed reducing units, geared motors and couplings; automotive and industrial forgings'. From small beginnings there appeared to be a good future, with a profit in 1960 of £615,730. But the Menzies credit squeeze of 1960–1961 interrupted that: 'already it has been necessary to retrench several hundred employees', the company reported in November 1960. In these adverse conditions, the company reported a profit of only £353,001 in 1961, but was back on track in 1962, reporting a profit of £730,476. 'The recovery', the company boasted, 'was an excellent achievement' — and a good time for Michael to be joining the company.

Thereafter, with Australia's infatuation with the car at ever-increasing levels, the phrase 'family car' gave way to 'the two car family', and more up-to-date models were needed every few years. By 1970, Borg-Warner stated that 'all divisions reported record turn-overs with increased market penetration and broader product coverage'. A new factory was opened at Albury on the New South Wales–Victoria border. In 1971, 'group sales were 22% higher'. In 1976, the two-millionth rear axle rolled off the production line at Yennora, suitably gold-plated. A decade later, the annual profit had reached $15.2 million.

Michael made a lucky move when he took a job at this rapidly expanding industrial enterprise, but it was an easy decision to make. He knew by now that he enjoyed factory work and could thrive in that environment. He could walk to work at Borg-Warner or cadge a lift with one of his workmates. It was about 1.5 kilometres from his front gate, or less than a 15 minute walk. The factory environment, if we rely on the photographs in the annual reports, was clean and modern with all the latest equipment, as befitted such an American giant. It was noisy, no doubt, and there was heavy work to be done. The great advantage in what seemed a continuous boom-time was that there was plenty of overtime.

There was a continuous, steady stream of work, and a man could see himself working there until he reached retirement age. The company seemed to like its workers and to look after them. Anyone who clocked up 25 years continuous employment at Borg-Warner received a gold watch and was eligible to join the 25 Year Club, whether they were still with Borg-Warner or accepting retirement on reaching that achievement. For the retirees, there was an annual reunion, where former workers could see how the company was faring and then attend a dinner, hosted by Borg-Warner, completely free and with all the trimmings. Though he fell just short of 25 years at Borg-Warner, as you will later see, Michael was made a member of the 25 Year Club on retirement, and attended the dinners shyly, but with a real measure of enjoyment.

But much of that is in the future. We were looking at this family in 1960, so let us return to that path. Anna works in her factory in Fairfield and is also well liked. Most of the women she works with speak Ukrainian, and they have become good friends. Anna has a kind heart and is deeply engaged with her small community. She likes to do good to all, and, when she and Michael entertain at home, she cooks up a storm. There must never be any sign of scrimping or saving on food — lavish would be the word to describe her hospitality.

Joe and Michalina are both doing well at school, and are happy children. They look forward eagerly to their annual holiday by the sea at Wollongong, where they stay with family friends for about a week. Michael doesn't own a car, so they travel to Wollongong by train, and, though the children never learn to swim, they love the beach and the water. Michalina was cross when Joe was given a bike, so her parents have bought her a piano. The children squabble as children will do. They have a dog, briefly, Buddy, and, as mature adults, they will still squabble over whose dog it really was. Both claim it as their own. Joe is beginning to play rugby league at school, and will develop into a talented local-grade footballer. Michalina already helps with the ironing and around the house, and will later play hockey and netball. There are plenty of children on the street, and there is always some kind of game going on. 'Aunty Tops' keeps an eye on all the children, but particularly looks out for Joe and Michalina until their mother comes home from work.

A salesman convinces Michael and Anna to buy land at Gwandalan on Lake Macquarie, on the Central Coast of New South Wales. They can build a holiday home there, he tells them, nothing too showy, but a lovely spot for when they come to retire. Retirement seems a long way off, but it's good to plan, so they do buy the land and eventually put a little cottage on it.

Michael begins to wonder if he can induce his younger brother, John, to come to Australia, to Fairfield. John is married now to Gina, and has two children, Lida and Bob. John and his family could take over the garage when they arrive until they find and can fund their own home. It would be good to have family around, and it's a mark of Michael's pleasure in his own migration, and in his confidence in Australia, that he urges John's migration. He is certain that John will have a much better life in Australia than in Poland. And so it comes to pass. Though

Michael begins the process of gaining visas and completing all the paperwork in 1960, the family doesn't arrive until 1961. Thereafter, the two families become very close.

There are uncertain times ahead for Australia, but, while unemployment suddenly becomes an issue in Australia as it has not been since the Second World War, Michael and Anna both keep their jobs. Michael admires the Liberal government of Robert Menzies, which has been in power almost since he arrived in Australia. He thinks back to the big strikes under Labor when they first arrived with amazement and annoyance. Neither he nor Anna vote, because they haven't yet become Australian citizens.

In June 1952, Anna — and, I presume, Michael and Joe, though I haven't seen their documents — received a Certificate of Authority to Remain in Australia. The certificate states 'that she is now entitled to remain here indefinitely subject to the laws of the Commonwealth'. On the reverse side, it states, 'As you will no doubt wish to become naturalised as an Australian Citizen and British subject, and so acquire the important privileges attaching to that status' she will need to bear in mind certain factors and will need, at some stage, to make a Declaration of Intention. The three of them, Michael, Anna, and Joe, become citizens in 1965, willing to accept all the obligations as thoughtful members of their adopted country. They each receive a small Bible for their trouble.

Michael does not take a close interest in politics, believing that Australia, so far away from everywhere, and so small in world terms, is as safe and secure as you could find. He dislikes unions because, when they impose a strike on his workplace, he loses money. He likes his bosses and believes that Borg-Warner is a good place to work. He would like to tell the unions to leave him and his co-workers alone; he is perfectly happy at work.

And so the years roll on in plenty of hard work, not only at

Yennora, but also in the vegie patch and garden at home. The children progress well at school, and both he and Anna never stop telling them of the importance of education. Maybe Michalina will become a schoolteacher — she was, after all, named for one of Anna's teachers at school — but that would mean university, and would they be able to afford it? Still, what an ambition. Michael would have liked to have been a teacher himself, and he was bright enough at school, but, really, it was out of the question. But look where life had taken him now. And Joe, what of Joe? He could go to university, too, but to study what? It will all work out in time, Michael is sure of that. For now, keep them keen on their schoolwork, and safe and happy at home.

But would somebody, the council, the government, please seal the road out the front? It's a quagmire in winter and so dusty in summer. It really isn't good enough. And still the night-cart man comes, when other people living in Sydney have sewerage. Fairfield should have that, too. So there are a few grizzles about life, and a few worries about the future, but, really, as Michael never tires of saying, 'so far, so good'.

Part Two

JOE'S STORY

A Problem to Start with

IT'S A SHOCKING AFFLICTION to lose your memory, as so many in our community can attest. Nursing a wife or a husband, a mother or a father with one of the several forms of dementia is so common now and among the hardest things a person can be called upon to do. So much of the person is lost, because we are who we are from our memories. I could tell you so much from my own past: about my parents and brothers, about my grandparents ('Barp' and Nana), about favourite uncles and aunties, liked cousins, family circumstances, school, Jesuits, going to the footy at South Melbourne. So much. These memories make me who I am.

We had better face up to the fact right at the beginning of this part of the narrative that, for almost all of his adult life, consequent on his shocking tragedy, Jaroslaw Stawyskyj, Joe as we all called him, had no short-term memory. None at all. Let me give you an example.

I mentioned the South Melbourne footy club above, my passion and my family's passion, too. South moved to Sydney in 1982, a forced move occasioned by too many years of failure. As the Sydney Swans, they were still my side, and just as passionately loved and followed. Joe knew this and asked me if he could go to a game with me, as he'd never seen Aussie Rules live. The club was terrific to us. Joe, you would need to know, had been in a wheelchair since his early 20s. A Swans staff member met us at the gate of the Sydney Cricket Ground, the Swans' home ground, as pre-arranged, escorted us to the elevator, showed us to our seats, and even gave us match-day programs. Joe seemed to have a great time. The Swans were playing St Kilda, and were in a purple patch of success, so were highly favoured to win. But they lost. After the game, we caught a taxi back to cousin Lida's place in Strathfield, where I had left the car, because it was simply easier to manoeuvre Joe in and out of the vehicle there than at the ground itself. We went through the back door of Lida's house, and everyone was keen to hear what Joe had made of his big day out. 'Who won?' they chorused. 'Western Suburbs', said Joe, naming a Sydney rugby league team with no connection at all to the game we had just watched. The actual game of Aussie Rules, less than an hour after its conclusion, had been entirely erased from his mind already.

So to tell you Joe's whole-of-life story presents a significant challenge. He could remember some things up to the time of his 'accident', but thereafter nothing stuck. Except names. If you had met him, perhaps only a few times, he would remember your name. Michalina introduced me into the family when Joe was about 40, maybe a bit younger. He had my name from the very beginning, somewhat elaborately pronounced as 'Mi-[long on the first syllable] cal [quick and brief on the second]'.

Joe could tell me something about his boyhood and his growing-up, but not too much. He remembered his schools, Our Lady of the Rosary and Patrician Brothers', but not down to the level of individual teachers or other students. He could tell you about his mum and dad and his great affection for them. He could tell you about his sister as a girl — clearly an annoying presence in his life — though with an underlying sense of deep care and pride. He could tell you about *his* dog, Buddy, not Michalina's dog, about his bike, his sport, playing rugby league at school and in the Catholic Youth competition, his job (well, a bit of it, anyway) after school, and he could remember the name of his girlfriend.

Michael had better memories of this time, as a father would, but they tend, of course, to be a father's memories. 'Oh, Joe was such a good boy', Michael would say. When Joe got his job, Michael said, he gave his mother all his wages, every payday, because he felt that was the right thing to do. Joe wanted them to have it a little easier, Michael reported, to have a bit more comfort in their lives, and he was very pleased to be adding to the family income. Joe was the first in the family to learn to drive, and, when Michael bought the first family car, Joe had almost complete charge of it until his father learned to drive. Joe was so good at sport, Michael claimed — though, had he ever seen Joe play a game of rugby league, I wondered. Joe had so many friends, Michael told me. Everybody liked him, and he was so good to the older people in the street. A father's memories, probably reliable, but far from the complete picture.

Joe's mother, Anna, would have had different, probably stronger, sharper, more-detailed memories. Her firstborn; her good, strong boy. Helpful, loving, doing his chores, giving her his money, taking burdens and responsibilities from her when he could. 'Such a good boy,' she might have said, 'he gave me no trouble at all.' Except that, because I never met Anna — she had died before I came on the scene — I have no access to those memories at all.

Nor can I turn to John, Joe's younger brother, of whom Joe was inordinately proud, for memories of Joe before the 'accident', because John was born in 1963 and has only the haziest memories of Joe before he became a soldier. Michalina can tell me more, as can Joe's aunty, but, again, these are outsider's accounts, faithful and loving, it's true, but who would rely on their aunty to tell their life story? So, reader, please be kind as we stumble together through this part of the story with very few records to guide us. We will do better later, when the record becomes more certain.

Pats Fairfield

WHO CAN SAY HOW MUCH school influences who we are and what we become? Attending a rare school reunion, since I hardly ever go to school reunions, I was shocked and surprised to hear bitter memories of a place I had remembered as happy and sympathetic. It was the 'cuts' (a belting with a firm leather strap) that left some of these former schoolboys aggrieved. A school may sustain and nurture us, it may prepare us for a future life, it may give us contacts and friendships that will shape the course of that life, or it may give us painful memories and a lifetime of difficulty and sadness. Like most of life, school can be a lottery.

Fairfield, and the west of Sydney generally, was growing rapidly in the early 1950s, causing headaches for all the planners and providers. What a strain it was: councils providing rudimentary roads and services to make blocks of land available, builders trying to keep up with the demand for housing, churches trying to put up new buildings to keep the people close to God, educators trying to cram bodies into classrooms …

For Catholics, schooling remained the overwhelming problem. Archbishops and bishops were running a massive school system on the backs of the faithful alone, without any form of government assistance, though Catholics paid their taxes, didn't they? This was and always had been a massive problem, and the Catholic school system was only possible because of the labour of an army of nuns and brothers who staffed the schools. Thirteen thousand of them, religious sisters and brothers, in the early years of the second half of the 20th century.

In 1952, the auxiliary archbishop of Sydney, Eris O'Brien, on behalf of cardinal Gilroy, wrote to the provincial (head) of the Patrician Brothers in Australia outlining a problem. Sydney was growing rapidly in the west, and, though there were Catholic churches out there, and priests, there were too few schools. The nearest boys' secondary school to Fairfield, a solid area of growth, was either at Parramatta or Granville, both too far away to be attractive to parents, and Granville didn't take boys through to the Leaving Certificate. Could the Brothers step in and run a school at Fairfield, archbishop O'Brien asked the Brother provincial.

A plot of land, a 'series of spent and uncultivated vineyards' of nine acres, had already been bought by the Church authorities surprisingly close to the town centre. A school block could be run up quickly, and an old house on the property could serve as the Brothers' monastery until a new one could eventually be built. The Brothers agreed to the request. Did they really have any alternative?

The Patrician Brothers, properly the Brothers of St Patrick, came into existence in 1808, in Ireland, as part of the great movement to reclaim Ireland for the Catholic Church. After many years of subjection to English rule, the Irish people were seriously adrift from their faith; they hardly knew even the basics. A massive program of teaching and learning was needed to rekindle the faith, and men and women were recruited into new religious congregations to provide the teachers. The Christian Brothers were the strongest manifestation of this new impulse, and came to dominate the scene, but, down in the diocese of Kildare and Leighlin, bishop Daniel Delany organised his own new institutes for men and women. The Sisters of St Brigid and the Brothers of St Patrick helped the bishop in his determination to educate his Catholic people. Both the Brigidines and the Patricians would play important roles in Australia.

The Patrician Brothers arrived in Australia in 1883, and were only ever a small presence in their new homeland, although, with few brothers, relative to the Christian Brothers, they ran a surprisingly large number of schools. They had opened a school at Blacktown in 1952, and would open at Liverpool in 1954. Their school at Fairfield, close to the railway line and the town centre, and with lots of land and a large population to draw on, was likely to be one of their biggest.

In 1953, when Patrician Brothers' College (Pats) Fairfield opened its doors to its first students, Joe Stawyskyj was just about to start in kindy at Our Lady of the Rosary, the parish school in Fairfield staffed by the Sisters of St Joseph. Boys at Rosary would transfer to Pats at the start of grade four according to the agreement knocked out at head office. This would relieve the nuns of swelling numbers and give the Brothers a guaranteed intake. In 1959, when Joe entered the senior school as a first year and began wearing long pants for the first time (a real step forward on the way to manhood), there were seven Brothers on the staff of the school, five of them young men, closer in age to the boys than to the boys' parents. There were five lay teachers, and a teacher-to-pupil ratio of one to 53. There were 56 boys in Joe's first-year class.

Teachers in these schools, and also in the state system, must have been made of stern stuff in the 1950s, as the population pressures became intense. The large numbers of students in each class increased discipline problems and meant there was limited opportunity for individual attention. Barry Greene at Patrician Brothers' Granville, who would transfer to Fairfield for his final two years of schooling in 1963, remembers a junior class at Granville of 60 students presided over by one teacher, Brother Augustine. Another class also used the same room, so that there were 100 boys in the one classroom. The school history insists 'this is not fiction'. Barry thought his teacher handled the class well, arranging the boys in rows based on achievement. Swift was the retribution if a boy faltered in his work — he would be moved across a row or two at least. Nor was there any relief for the teachers from teaching during any period of the day, with no time allowed in a staff room for preparation of classes or for marking. All of this was done after school hours.

Many of the Brothers spoke with an Irish accent, which means that they had been recruited and trained from their homes in Ireland and sent to the Australian mission, usually for the remainder of their lives. In April 1961, the Brothers opened their new, long-planned monastery at Fairfield. Before that, the ratio of bedrooms to Brothers in the old farmhouse was four to nine, with two Brothers missing out on a bedroom entirely. One of these two slept in a corridor and one slept in the parlour, his makeshift bed only available to him when the last guest at the monastery left or the last meeting for the night was over.

The Brothers wore Roman collars, though cut down in size to distinguish them from priests, with black cassocks covering black pants, and black shoes, and, if they were finally professed, a dark-green sash worn around the waist and then running vertically to the ground along the side of the right leg. Black in Sydney's long months of heat may not have been sensible or sympathetic. To a small boy, it may have appeared confronting. But spare a thought for Brother Aengus or Brother Luke. Sleeping in a corridor by night, permanently in a classroom of 53 or more boys by day, and with all the prayers, religious observances, and deprivations to be fitted in, too.

1959 was a good year for Joe. He was in First Year Blue, of which his teacher, Brother Mark, wrote: 'children of many lands combined to make First Year Blue into a responsible class, ambitious to do well, both in the present and in the future, and willing to learn'. Of the ten prefects at the school in 1959, only two had what we might call Anglo-Celtic names, Stevenson and Fitzgerald. We may assume that these boys mingled happily with Kolodynski, Kotulski, Zgolak, and Pospisil, among others. Joe was dux of First Year Blue. The boys studied religion, Brother Mark wrote of his class for the school's annual magazine, *The Rosarian*, 'and came to envy Adam when they discovered he lived at a time when there were no school teachers'. They also studied algebra, geometry, chemistry, physics, history ('all were quick to realise that the Ice Age did not immediately precede the Refrigerator Age'), and English.

Joe dropped down to 31st in the class in 1960, which was a big drop from his previous high achievement. Kindly Brother Mark wrote that 'Joe's position in class may seem low but he has a subject less than the other boys. His marks show weakness in English and Geography to which he should pay more attention if he wants to increase his class position. In general however his work is good.' His conduct was 'very good', his application was 'good', his attendance 'regular', and his 'neatness and dress … very good'. A fellow student in Joe's year remembered that Joe wasn't academic or naturally scholarly, but he agreed with Joe's teachers that Joe worked hard and was always co-operative in class.

In 1961, there was a record 490 boys in the primary school and 428 in the secondary school. Joe was Third Year Gold alongside 53 others. There were 15 teachers on the staff, including eight Brothers. Joe was not yet in the cadets, organised by a Brother, and was yet to appear in school-sports photographs. He gained the Intermediate Certificate in 1961. The school was still growing strongly in 1962, with 493 primary students and 515 secondary students. Unless there is a mistake in the printed class lists in *The Rosarian*, and that seems unlikely, Joe repeated Third Year Gold in 1962 and again gained the Intermediate Certificate. If he did repeat, I can't explain why. Perhaps the Brothers thought he was too young yet for the final years of schooling. He played in the Open Grade rugby league team, which reached the grand final of its competition, but lost that game narrowly to Ryde. There was a B Grade and an A Grade above Open Grade.

In 1963, Joe was in Fourth Year B, and won a prize for being top in religion, but he didn't make the top three in his class on the academic list. There were now only 34 boys in his fourth-year class. Barry Greene chose to continue his schooling to the Leaving Certificate, transferring schools to do so. He had worked in the Granville post office, in a summer job, sorting mail, and decided there had to be more to life than this. The motivation of other boys may have been similar. It was just understood at home that Joe would complete his schooling. This was not negotiable. Pats Fairfield had only started teaching to the Leaving Certificate level in 1961, but Joe would go right through to the end.

Joe was a member of the B Grade rugby league team in 1963, and was also a member of the combined-athletics team. Already, Pats Fairfield had developed a reputation as a sporty school and was making its presence felt in the various competitions in which teams were entered. Joe was a highly skilled and high-achieving athlete, thought to be the fastest or equal-fastest boy in the school at a variety of distances, though Joe believed that a boy named Juliani was faster than he was. Joe was quick, too, on the football field, and, though of slight build, was a well-regarded member of his teams. A lay teacher, Kevin Bourke, who taught mathematics, was also the football and athletics coach, and Joe spent long hours in training under Mr Bourke's care. The boys were well drilled, and gained confidence from their success. 'We believed in ourselves', was how Barry Greene described it. The school had good facilities for sport, including very good ovals.

Joe joined the cadets, probably in 1962, under Brother Mark and

Brother Aengus, who, for cadet purposes, were known as Lieutenant Ryan and Lieutenant Kavanagh. A fellow cadet who was Joe's platoon sergeant said that Joe liked the cadets, but there was little to it other than marching and some rifle drill. Brother Charles, perhaps with a wry sense of humour, referred to the Pats Fairfield cadets as the 'Polish Army'.

The boys had begun to notice the girls at neighbouring schools as they matured, and teachers arranged dances and other opportunities for socialising. Pictures of the school dances in *The Rosarian* make them look pretty drab affairs, but those were the times. At the beginning of 1963, Joe turned 16 years of age. He was good looking, had fair hair, was quite tall, and had the build of a good athlete: spare and rangy.

A term report from 1963, which has survived among his papers, noted that Joe's conduct remained 'very good', as did his application, neatness, and attendance. But he was 21st in the class in that report on his second term's work, and Brother Luke wrote, 'this has NOT been a good term ... these marks MUST improve'. This seems a bit tough since Joe scored 72 for religion, 70 for English, and 66 for history. General science at 49 and economics at 55 let him down, but he rounded out well with 68 in geography. Standards must have been pretty high at Pats, or perhaps his teachers saw a higher ability in Joe than he was currently achieving. A reader looking at these reports today would focus more on Joe's good conduct and good attendance as an indicator of character rather than his marks, which might move up or down, depending on his motivation. Barry Greene said that Joe was a quiet boy at school who did not seek to stand out from the crowd. He was popular and well liked, with a very pleasant smile when a remark or joke tickled his fancy.

In 1964, just turning 17, Joe entered his final year of schooling, studying for his Leaving Certificate. He was also in the A Grade rugby league team and again in the combined-athletics team, still with a heavy load of training and games. The curriculum had undergone change as New South Wales schools prepared for the implementation of the Wyndham Scheme, which, in a couple of years, would add an extra year of schooling for all students who wished to matriculate. The published results in the newspapers show that Joe earned two As and three Bs in the Leaving Certificate. This is a creditable result, but he failed in mathematics. His As were in modern history and economics. Looking at the results for his Pats contemporaries, of whom 41 gained the Leaving Certificate in 1964, Joe's marks are average. Two or three As was typical for Pats, and most boys earned passes in five or six subjects. Very few reached honours level in any of the subjects, though a few H1s and H2s were awarded to Pats boys. No one boy stood out at Pats that year with a very high score.

At least it was now all over, the routine and regimen of school. Many former students can remember walking out of school for the last time. It was a bittersweet moment: pleasure at release, perhaps, but regret, too, for the friendships forged that may now be broken, and for the sense of achievement that the group, the class year, had made it through to the end, had progressed in knowledge and maturity. Strong, too, was a sense of anticipation for the future. But the pattern and rhythm of life for 11 or 12 years was now disrupted, the safety net of school gone forever, and there was a sense that the now former school students, though not entirely on their own, were, at least and at long last, now more responsible for their own lives than they had ever been. The future was theirs to make.

Barry Greene borrowed a mate's suit for an interview at the ANZ Bank, but was offered a teacher's scholarship beforehand, so he cancelled the interview. As he waited for his exam results, Joe looked at his life with a sense of excitement for a new beginning. He did attend an interview at ANZ, and, to his great delight, was offered a position, on the bottom rung. Work, sport, adventure, and — perhaps — romance beckoned, and Joe was ready to embrace it all.

New Arrivals

MICHAEL'S YOUNGER BROTHER, Ivan, the youngest child in the family, was born on 2 June 1929. So he was just ten years of age when Michael, then 17, was taken to work for the Germans in Sudetenland. Ivan would never see his elder brother at home again. Yet Michael never forgot the younger boy. Some time in 1960, Michael wrote to Ivan from his home in Fairfield telling him of the pleasures and opportunities of life in Australia.

Ivan had married Eugenia (Gina) Maleck in 1955, and there were two children, Lida (born in 1957) and Robert (Bob or Bobbie, born in 1959). Ivan had a hard life working to provide for his family, driving a semi-trailer logging truck in and out of a Polish forest. He had left his parents' farm and now lived in a city, which is probably why Michael felt it was safe to write to him, because there was greater anonymity in the cities. Michael told me that, except for his letter to say goodbye, he had never written to his mother after the war ended, for fear that he would put her into trouble with the communist authorities. He most certainly did not want to do that.

Ivan's first thought on receiving Michael's letter was to think he might travel to Sydney alone to see for himself if life in Australia was just as his brother had described it. Anna, in Fairfield, was having none of that. Ivan and his family would come to Sydney as a family, as migrants, or not at all, she insisted to Michael. Ivan could raise GB£100 for the cost of the travel; Michael borrowed a part of the remainder from a church group, and chipped in the rest from his own savings. All up, the journey cost Ivan's family GB£500, which was a very considerable amount of money at the time.

The family sailed from Genoa on the Lloyd Triestino Line MS *Australia*, which came into service on 21 May 1950. Photographs of *Australia* show a cramped and crowded ship — in tourist class, anyway. Gina was sick all the way to Sydney and hated every minute of the voyage. They arrived in port on 29 August 1961.

Then there was confusion at the dockside. Michael had arranged for his family to be allowed to go on board to search for the newcomers, but, while they were in the office organising the permissions, John (as Ivan would henceforth be known), Gina, Lida, and Bob had stepped for the first time onto Australian soil. So the hosts were on board and the new arrivals on the land, each eagerly searching for the other group. Eventually, they all met up and great was the rejoicing. Anna's boss had arranged for two cars to be waiting to take the immigrants back to Fairfield.

Michael and Anna had redecorated the garage, where the new family would live for the foreseeable future. They had repapered the walls and spruced things up, but it was a garage and therefore still quite primitive. For displaced persons, the garage — built by themselves, no less — had been a step up; for city folk looking for a better life, it was difficult. There was no toilet or bathroom, said Gina, and only a tiny cooking alcove; but there were enough beds and space to relax. It was agreed that Gina would cook in Anna's kitchen for both families, at least until Christmas, while John, Michael, and Anna would work. Michael found work for John with him at Concord. The newcomers had arrived on a Thursday, and John went to work for the first time the following Monday. Like Michael, John took all the overtime offered and saved every penny he could. That's why they were living in the garage, to save and save and save to pay off the travel costs and then to start saving for their own home.

Gina admitted that she found it difficult to adjust to her new homeland. She had no English at all, and didn't find people particularly friendly or welcoming. 'We came from a communist country,' she said, 'so people thought we were communists, and they were suspicious of us and very reluctant to deal with us.' Yet, even then, she could see, she said, that they would have a better future in Australia than in Poland. Better for them and much better for their children. John was less sure, greatly missing his old life and his old friends. He often talked about going back home.

It was strange for Joe and Michalina suddenly to have, for the first time, an uncle and an aunt and cousins. They ate together and shared the chores, but Joe and Michalina still had their own lives, their schools, their school friends, their sport, for Joe the scouts, and they were well at home in their suburb, their city, and their country. Nevertheless, Joe did as much as he could for the newcomers, and became especially close to his aunty. He went with her to the shops and carried the shopping home, chatted to her about Australian ways and his own interests, and shared as much as he could. Lida and Bob were too young to play with Joe, but Michalina enjoyed having her cousins around and often played with them.

There seemed now to be more of a sense of family; they were more like other Australian extended families, not the four of them alone in the world. Even so, it was a little difficult for Michael and Anna to watch the newcomers trying to settle in. When John grumbled that maybe they would be better off back home in Poland, Anna told Gina that, if her husband did go, she should remain in Sydney with her children; she and Michael would do what they could to help her as a single mother.

John did return to Poland, but soon recognised the error of his ways and came quickly back to his family. He bought land at Yennora, quite close to Fairfield, in 1965, and found a builder who could put up the home in six to eight months. John, Gina, Lida, and Bob were ready to move into their new home at the end of 1965, after more than four years in the garage at Bell Crescent.

In the meantime, there were other new arrivals on the scene. Joe and Michalina found that they were to have a new baby in their family, and, in August 1963, their brother John was born. Then Gina became pregnant again, and Stephen was born in 1965 during the last months in the garage. Joe, by this stage, had already left school and was working in the bank.

Life had proved eventful at Bell Crescent. Anna had left full-time work after John's birth and was now preparing again for life at home with just her own family. But they would remain close, the two families, so long separated and then so intimately connected for several years. Michael much enjoyed having his brother alongside him. Life seemed so good again.

The Bank

TO MATRICULATE TO UNIVERSITY at the end of his school years, Joe needed a minimum of two As, which he had, and a minimum of five passes, which he had also obtained. So university was a possibility that Joe must have considered. The range of courses he could have chosen had narrowed, however, because he did not have a pass in maths: the heavier degrees — engineering, science, economics — were not available to him. Whether this influenced his thinking, we can't now know. If Joe had gone straight on to university as he turned 18 in 1965, he would have completed a three-year degree in time to be available for conscription to the Australian army at the age of 21. But the completion of his studies would have deferred his service for at least six months. This might have been crucial.

Joe decided not to go to university, opting, instead, for a career in commerce. Looking at the pages of the newspapers where the Leaving Certificate results for all New South Wales students were published, I was astonished by the number of advertisements from the several banks then in existence. Banks must have been looking to recruit many young people who had completed the Leaving but who could not afford or were not interested in higher study. At that time, just 3 per cent of the Australian workforce had a university degree, so the route Joe took was not unusual — indeed, it was the norm. Joe found a job with the Australia and New Zealand Bank Ltd, Chief Manager's Office, 2 Martin Place, Sydney. He would be a teller and would learn his craft.

Michael explained that Joe felt a real sense of responsibility to his parents, and wanted to contribute. Both parents had long been in steady factory employment close to home. Joe strongly admired both of them for their hard work and the success they had made of their lives in Australia. Both had good jobs, though Anna had now retired to care for John; both worked very hard at their factories and at home, caring and providing diligently for the family. Joe was conscious that he had been a burden to his parents for all his years of schooling. He was denied nothing that he needed. There were the extras, too. A good bike for getting around the suburb to see his friends, sporting equipment, and toys. Eventually, there had been a television, a big expenditure in those days, though they still had no car. Joe knew that his father was careful with his money and had managed it successfully, debt-free when a mortgage was a reality for most in Fairfield, as elsewhere in the suburbs. Joe also knew that his parents had worked hard to settle Uncle John and his family in Australia.

Joe wanted to contribute, to make a real difference in his parents' lives, as soon as he could. After all, there was still his little brother, John, to raise and educate, a toddler at only three years of age. So when Joe received his first pay packet from the ANZ Bank, without being urged to, or it being spoken of with him, he handed it, unopened, to his mother, who gave him, from it, what she thought he would need for his living expenses. He continued to do this as long as he worked at the bank and lived at home. 'Oh, Joe was a good boy', Michael always said.

Joe had several postings with the bank, in the City, at Parramatta, elsewhere in Sydney. He liked the work and was good at it. He also liked his work colleagues, and really liked the independence of work as opposed to the discipline of the classroom. Somehow, probably from a mate, Joe learned to drive, and Michael bought a car, the family's first, which Joe taught him to drive. But, initially, Joe was the family driver, and he loved it. He loved the freedom that driving gave him, and, away from Bell Crescent, he was probably a bit of a 'mug lair'. At least, that's the way he liked to present himself later in life.

Joe had enjoyed sport at school and was good at it, so it was no surprise that he would want to keep on playing rugby league football. Training twice a week, matches on Sundays throughout the winter, plenty of mates, plenty of fun. Better than sitting at a desk at night studying, what, history? So Joe joined the Catholic Youth Organisation (CYO) at Merrylands, just down the road, as soon as he could, and really enjoyed his footy.

Though the CYO boasted that 'our sporting services for girls and young men are easily the largest competitions in the Commonwealth [of Australia]', it intended to be a great deal more than that. Writing in its handbook, cardinal Gilroy explained that the CYO 'has the task of winning youth to the standard of Christ the King'. He also explained that it was 'intended for all young Catholics ... right to the very day of their marriage'. The CYO itself claimed that it 'has the vital task of helping youth to prepare for marriage'. It was, indeed, an excellent means by which many young Catholics found partners for marriage, and might have been seen as a kind of marriage market.

CYO members were expected to attend Mass and take Communion on Sundays and on one other day during the week as well. Joe was certainly diligent in his Sunday observance, but he would rarely have attended weekday Mass. How diligent he was in the spiritual side of the CYO life is not now known, but, throughout his life, he showed no sign of being anything other than an observant, obedient, and believing Catholic. So the CYO would have supported and nurtured his faith.

The CYO certainly satisfied his sporting inclinations. There was a nice team photo of Joe and his teammates in their Merrylands CYO footy gear in the family living room for all the time that Michael remained in the house he had built. The boys were stripped and ready for action, and were a good-looking group of blokes into the bargain. Joe took great satisfaction from his time with the Merrylands footy team, and stayed with it in the years before he joined the army. His attachment to the team was a part of who he was.

Joe met his girlfriend, Maria, at the CYO as well. They were 'going steady', in the language of the time, and showed a real affection for each other. The organisation handbook had predicted that 'if you give your time and talent generously to the work of the CYO, you will get from it, for yourself, the things you want — firm friends, enjoyment, the precious security of growing to maturity with the help and guidance the Church alone can give you'. Both Maria and Joe were growing to maturity, but only they would know if they talked much at all about the future. It was the beginning of a relationship, Joe's first, and both Joe and Maria moved slowly into this new territory. Maria was not a frequent visitor at Bell Crescent. There was no thought of Joe moving in with Maria, as might be more the norm now. In those days, and in the Ukrainian community particularly, young men and young women lived with their parents until they were married. Only then did they set up their own homes, and Joe would have accepted that as part of the natural order of things. Nevertheless, he and Maria spent a fair bit of time together, often in the company of other mates, though, again, this time was likely spent somewhat differently than it would be today.

Rule 22 of the CYO's quite extensive list of rules may not have been popular with all members of the organisation: 'alcoholic liquor is forbidden at CYO functions of every description. This applies particularly to men's sporting teams', including even after training runs. I imagine the rule was observed, because, if broken, the diocesan CYO officials had the power to suspend an entire team from its relevant competition. No doubt the young men on the team, and their supporters, found other places where they might celebrate their wins and drown their sorrows.

Joe couldn't finish the 1967 rugby league competition with his CYO teammates, because he was required to report to the army on 12 July, towards the end of the season, with the finals to be played in August. He said his goodbyes to Maria and his mates in the strong hope that he might resume this enjoyable life as soon as his stint in the army was over. They all hoped to see him back soon, and wished him good luck and all the best.

Unique in Australian History

JUST AS JOE WAS FINISHING his schooling in 1964, the prime minister and his government in Canberra were taking decisions that would have the most profound effect on the future course of Joe's life, though Joe little realised it at the time. On 10 November 1964, prime minister Robert Menzies announced the introduction of a compulsory 'national service' scheme for service in the Australian army.

It was not to be a universal scheme, but would involve only a part of Australia's young manhood. The first intake, of those who would turn 20 years of age in the first six months of 1965, would consist of 4,200 men, or about one in 20 of all Australian young men obliged to register for service. One young man would go into the army for full-time service; 19 others would continue with the lives they had begun to shape. This was a huge burden on some and of no consequence at all to those who were not called up — the scheme was totally unfair and unequal.

There had been no debate in Parliament or in the community about the scheme, no testing of the acceptance of the scheme at an election, and no referendum on conscription as prime minister Billy Hughes had ordered in 1916 and 1917. The government wanted conscription to bolster failing army recruitment, and one in 20 young men just had to cop it. At this stage, it was not announced that these young men would be going to foreign wars, but the scheme did allow that they might serve overseas.

Under the scheme that Menzies announced, each young man, in his 20th year, was obliged to register with the Commonwealth Department of Labour and National Service. It was illegal not to register, and Joe wouldn't willingly break the law. Draft resisters, or 'draft dodgers' as they were labelled — that is, those who did not register — received prominence in the newspapers and on television, but, in reality, they were quite small in number. Who can know what was in Joe's mind as he submitted his registration papers? Like most young men, he probably thought, 'Well, it can't happen to me, but, if I am conscripted, well, perhaps I will have to take my medicine.' Send off the form and let's see what happens. There was argument in the community, and some of the draft resisters stepped up in public to argue against conscription, but the overwhelming majority of 20-year-old men in Australia followed the law and registered for the ballot.

At this point, the scheme became unusual, perhaps even weird — or, as some might say, deeply offensive. The department asked for the help of Australia's largest lottery company, the Melbourne-based Tattersall's (many people in those days in Victoria and elsewhere took a regular 'ticket in Tatts'), to operate a lottery to find the conscripts. Twice a year, the department would conduct a ballot drawing out from the Tattersall's lottery barrel, with numbers representing days of the month for each of the six months under consideration. Young men born on those dates were to be conscripted into the army; all others were excused service. Conscripts were required to serve in the Australian Regular Army, full-time, for two years, to be followed by three years part-time service in the Australian Citizen Military Force (the army reserve).

I was a participant in the first ballot because I turned 20 on 10 April 1965. The ballot was held in Melbourne, at the Tattersall's lottery office in Flinders Street, on 10 March 1965, exactly one month before my birthday. Although there was always a senior politician presiding at the ballot, and the marbles were drawn out of the barrel by a person of some prominence or celebrity — on one occasion by former Australian test-cricket captain Lindsay Hassett — the dates of those to be excluded or included were not published. The lottery was not open to members of the public as the very regular Tattersall's draws were. Indeed, the normal Tatts draws were then a part of the entertainment that Melbourne offered. But the room was closed and barred for the conscription lottery. The dates, though not published, were retained in the government records and are now available to be studied. At the time, however, all those who entered the ballot had no idea of success or failure in the ballot itself, and relied on a letter they would receive from the department within a week or two of the ballot, telling of their deferral or their conscription.

The dates drawn out for the April that interested me were: 1, 3, 4, 6, 7, 8, 11, 13, 14. As the department had no idea how many would seek exemption or deferment once conscripted or how many would fail the medical examination, many more dates were drawn in the early lotteries than would be drawn later. For those born in April 1945, 16 dates from the 30 available were drawn. As 10 April was not one of these dates, I received a letter, dated 24 March 1965, from the Department of Labour and National Service, National Service Registration Office, advising me that my 'liability to render service … has been indefinitely deferred'. 'You may therefore take it', the letter continued, 'that you will not be called up for service under the present arrangements.'

Though the address lines of the letter contained only six words, the department managed to make two mistakes in attempting to render my name ('McKermam', and a mistake with the second of my Christian names, which is not 'Matthews') and one mistake with my address. Three mistakes within six words did not give much confidence in the management of this complex scheme. The department advised me to keep the letter safe, 'as it provides evidence of your deferment', and I have retained it to the present day, just in case.

Joe Stawyskyj was born on 17 January 1947, and was therefore entered in the fifth ballot held at the lottery offices, on 11 March

1967. As we know now, but he did not know then, 11 dates were drawn for January: 1, 4, 6, 7, 12, 16, 17, 20, 24, 25, 30. He did not, therefore, receive a letter such as I had earlier received; instead, he received a letter telling him when and where to report for a medical examination, and when and where to report for duty in the Australian army. He had lost in a ballot that would profoundly affect his life, as it would destroy the lives of 185 national servicemen killed on the field of battle in Vietnam, and touch the lives of many hundreds wounded or in other ways damaged. A ballot seems such a cruel way to determine the fate of 20-year-old boys. Boys, it might be added, who could not yet vote.

The scheme allowed for some exemptions and deferments of those called-up. If you were a married man, you would be 'deferred indefinitely'. Having submitted your registration for national service, and having participated in the ballot, and having been called-up, you still had a couple of months in which you had time to marry and claim the exemption. But what young man would marry simply as a means of avoiding conscription? Perhaps there were a few, but most would not have even thought of it.

Students and apprentices could seek a temporary deferment, but they would be eligible for national service when they had completed their course of study. Advised in late March of your conscription in the lottery, it was then too late to enrol at a university and apply for a temporary deferment. So this route was closed to all who were not currently in studies or apprenticeships.

Permanently exempt were 'persons with prescribed physical and mental disabilities', and we all heard plenty of stories at the time of the lengths to which some had resorted to give evidence of some sort of disability. How many of the stories were true, it would be impossible to say, but there must have been some who attempted a scam of one sort or another.

Permanently exempt, too, so long as they maintained their current status, were theological students, ministers of religion (at 20 years of age?), and members of religious orders. This provision may have been a throwback to the strong opposition argument in the 1917 conscription-referendum campaign from members of the Australian Catholic hierarchy. Billy Hughes omitted to exclude members of religious orders and theological students from his list of exemptions for the proposed conscription scheme of 1917, and the Catholic bishops chose to take this as an attack on their church and their schools. It freed them to campaign aggressively against conscription. Menzies wanted no such issue to arise now. All those young men in seminaries, novitiates, and training houses could continue their lives in peace and security, and lend their support, if they chose, to the government's harsh measures. Certainly, this time around, most Catholic leaders strongly supported national service.

Finally, we come to the question of conscientious objection. A permanent exemption could be gained by young men 'who satisfy a Court of their conscientious objection'. The National Service Act specified that a conscientious objection must be based on an objection to all war on the grounds of religious belief — no other grounds would be accepted, and the objection must be to all war, not to a specific war. Crown prosecutors would soon be asking young men about their understanding of Hitler and the Nazis, about reactions if enemy soldiers were seen raping their sisters and their mothers, and all sorts of other lurid stories aimed at seeking agreement from the applicant that war and violence might be necessary as a consequence of extreme events. Very few young Australian men were ever able to successfully satisfy a court of their conscientious objection.

I can't say if Joe thought of any of these options when he received the letter telling him that he was liable to render national service. But, in truth, there were very few options available to him. He wasn't studying or in an apprenticeship. He suffered no physical or mental disability — indeed, he continued to play rugby league and was in excellent health. Though he regularly attended his church and had done well in religious studies at school, he had not formed a conscientious objection to war, and, despite the impact of war on the lives of both his parents, he would have strongly supported the need to defeat the regime that had made slaves of both his mother and his father. He and Maria were not married, and he would never have thought of marriage so lightly as a means of escaping his fate. Obviously, he wasn't a member of a religious order, nor was he willing to avail himself of any of the means that had been designed to placate the churches.

It wasn't like the last time when members of this family had experienced conscription. Troops hadn't marched into Bell Crescent to take one male from each family for the service of the state at war. (Though, even in Australia in the late 1960s, police would have become involved if Joe had refused to accept his fate; he would have been arrested and imprisoned.) This time, it was a matter of forms and letters and marbles in a barrel. But was the consequence really that different? The Nazi state asserted then that it could take control of the life and the labour of one of its subjects. That it could take away from him his power to determine his own fate, take away his ability to use his own freedom to create the life for himself that he wished to lead. That he could be compelled to live a life according to the rules and whims of others, to do as he was told, to go where he was ordered, to surrender his will and interests to the will and interests of those he served.

Michael and Anna had seen all this before. Michael's older brother had been conscripted into the Polish army; Michael had volunteered himself into the charge of Slovakian troops to make the long journey to Sudetenland and an unknown fate. Anna, too, had been taken from her family, whom she was never to see again, and forced to labour, without pay, where she was directed and how. She could not choose where she might go, what she might eat, where she might sleep.

Joe would, of course, be less like his parents and more like the uncle he had never met. He was subject to the rule of Australian and army law. He would be paid for his service in the army, and would accrue benefits if he were to serve overseas. His length of service was prescribed and would not exceed two years full-time. He would have time off and freedom of movement when not on duty. His standard of living would not differ vastly from what he had known at home for all his life. He would be well enough fed, well housed and warm, though living communally, and would be playing sport, drinking with his mates, and generally living it up when he could, like any other normal 21-year-old Australian male.

But for Anna and Michael, perhaps even for Joe, there was fear in the back of their minds. Life is shaped by those who control you. Joe would pass out of their care, out of their sight, as they had passed out of their parents' care and their parents' sight. There was every cause for concern.

The Call-up

HAROLD EDWARD HOLT WAS ELECTED leader of the parliamentary Liberal Party in Canberra on 20 January 1966, replacing Sir Robert Menzies, knighted in 1963 and who retired on 26 January 1966. Holt became Australia's 17th prime minister, having waited in the wings for more than a decade. Holt is largely remembered for the manner of his death — drowned while swimming off Portsea's Cheviot Beach. He's also remembered for his almost pathetic subservience to the Americans. Holt came up with the awful slogan 'All the way with LBJ' while speaking in Washington in late June 1966. When US president Lyndon Baines Johnson visited Sydney, Melbourne, and Canberra in October 1966, Holt continued to use this deplorable slogan. The Australian prime minister seemed to have a special rapport with Johnson, but, as a formulation of national policy, his slogan was fawning and embarrassing.

Holt significantly escalated Australia's involvement in the war in Vietnam. He raised Australia's contribution to the war three times in his 23 months in office, sending an additional 3,000 troops to Vietnam. Many of these troops would be conscripts, for Holt had no intention of abandoning his predecessor's contentious policy of conscripting 20-year-old Australian males for service in the army. But the Australians that the government was conscripting were quite a different bunch from the soldiers that had served Australia in the two world wars.

In September 1967, Holt welcomed to Canberra the first president of Italy to visit Australia, Giuseppe Saragat. There were riotous scenes of enjoyment and celebration, particularly in Melbourne, but also in Sydney and Canberra. Described as 'a Roman Carnival' to do honour to the visitor, especially among the Italian community, the occasion became, in fact, a celebration of the role of migrants in the Australian community and the role of immigration in recent Australian history. Those welcoming president Saragat gave considerable recognition in their speeches to the role that post-war immigration had played in changing the face of modern Australia.

Australia in the late 1960s was a much different country than it had been immediately after the war. In the intervening time, nearly 2.5 million people had migrated to Australia, and the population had increased from seven million to more than 12 million. Over 300,000 people had migrated from Italy — more than from any other country except Britain. By 1967, one-third of the Italian migrants had been naturalised; that is, they had taken Australian citizenship, confirming themselves as Australians, prepared to play a full part in the development of their new country. It had always been a part of Australia's immigration program that the new arrivals would eventually take out citizenship and commit themselves permanently to Australia.

Among the Stawyskyj family records, there are three identical Bibles, published by the British and Foreign Bible Society, and printed for the society by the Cambridge University Press. The Bibles were a gift from the society to Michael, Anna, and Joe, who each took out Australian citizenship at a ceremony at the Fairfield Municipal Council on 20 May 1965. Joe was then 18 years of age, old enough to know his own mind. Perhaps his parents had waited to become naturalised until Joe was old enough to make his own choice. Michalina didn't need to take part in the ceremony, as she had been born in Australia, at Bathurst in 1950, and was, therefore, Australian.

Menzies had reintroduced conscription six months before Joe took out citizenship. The government, aware of the large number of migrant children in the Australian population, concluded that it would be deeply divisive if Australian-born males were to be conscripted while those born overseas would be ineligible. Conscription therefore applied equally to Australian-born males and to overseas-born males residing in Australia, so that Joe's act of loyalty to his adopted country was irrelevant in deciding his fate as a conscript. Joe would commence his two-year service in the Australian army in July 1967, a little more than two years after he had become a citizen.

His Aunty Gina remembers that Joe was unhappy at the news, and somewhat angry, too. This was not how he had imagined his life developing. He would be leaving his mother and father's home, saying goodbye to his sister and to his brother, who was not yet even at school. Saying goodbye to Maria and his mates, leaving the work he liked and in which he hoped to make his career, to be a part of an organisation he had never thought of joining voluntarily.

Did Joe have any room to move? Any way at all of avoiding the obligation that the government had imposed upon him? Gina thought that he had. She was very close to Joe; she loved him very much, she told me. Gina was then pregnant with her third child — even so, she still joined her husband, and Anna and Michael, in working on the block of land that John had bought and where he would soon build his and her first house. They had been clearing the block one day, in hard physical toil, and had all come back home for dinner and rest, when Gina began to experience the first labour pains. It was Joe who drove Gina to the hospital; Joe who talked through Gina's admission, as she didn't yet speak much English. So Joe and Gina were close.

She sat down with him after he had announced the news of his conscription, and she hatched a plan. In the time remaining before he had to present himself to the army, she said, Joe should make a visit to his grandmother and her family in Poland. The old woman was still alive, and still remembered fondly her dear boy Michael and his family, though she had never, of course, even seen Anna or the children, and had not seen Michael since his departure for Sudetenland in the first months of the war so many years ago. The old woman would be delighted to welcome Joe to the home and the farm, Gina told Joe, and there would certainly be work for him either on the farm or in the district. He could stay there, Gina advised, until all this dreadful conscription business was over. And then he could come home and get on with his life.

The plan was possible, and perhaps some other migrant boys did do this. Plenty of American boys, facing similar prospects, fled to Canada. But after careful thought, Anna and Michael advised Joe against Gina's plan. There were too many risks involved in breaking the law in this way — and would Joe ever be allowed to participate fully as an Australian if he defied the law and refused to perform his national-service obligation? He might be arrested on his return home from Poland, to face who knew what fate. So Joe rejected Gina's advice, though he might well have been tempted by it. He would accept his obligation for service, and he would try to get through it as honourably and as successfully as possible, promising his parents that he would always try to remain safe and sound.

Basic Training

2787617 PRIVATE JARSLOW STAWYSKYJ (the army permanently dropped the 'o' from Jaroslaw) joined the Australian Regular Army Supplement (National Service) on 12 July 1967. He was 20 and a half years of age.

There are two pictures in the family's photograph albums that deserve close inspection. The first is of Joe, his sister, and ten mates. They are in the living room at Bell Crescent. On a table in the foreground is a vinyl record, so there was music. All the boys have drinks in their hands; some hold bottles. Joe is holding a clear bottle with clear liquid. It may be vodka. Michalina is wearing a winter dress, and most of the boys have jackets, cardigans, or jumpers. It is winter. July, we assume. This, we think, is Joe's 'going away' party. Certainly Joe's hair is cut much closer than any of the other boys, so perhaps he had taken a precautionary pre-army haircut. They are a happy group — smiling, of course, for the camera — but relaxed and informal. Clearly all good mates. Footy mates? Work mates? Former school mates? Perhaps a bit of each.

The second photo is more formal. There is a table at which guests are seated. Joe, Michalina, and their mother stand in front of a highly decorated cake. Joe and Michalina look confidently at the camera; Anna looks wistfully at Joe. There's a bit of bunting in the background; this is a big celebration. It's Joe's 21st birthday party, and he's been in the army now for more than six months. He has filled out more, and is much more mature-looking, perhaps even hardened, than he had been in the photo seven months earlier. He holds a cake knife in one hand and a tall beer stein in the other (he was born in Germany, after all). Joe has either spoken and will cut the cake, or he is about to speak. Perhaps he laughs a bit about the army and his current service. Perhaps he joshes those who are not defending their country as he is. Perhaps he admits that he can't wait for his army days to be over so that he can get back to work in the bank. Whatever he did say is lost to us now. But it was a good night, enjoyed by all.

Some 800,000 young men registered for national service during the existence of the scheme, from 1964 to 1972; 63,735 were called up to spend two years full-time in the army. The new recruits were given ten weeks of basic training at one of three recruit-training battalions in Australia: 1 Recruit Training Battalion, at Kapooka, near Wagga Wagga in southern New South Wales; 3RTB, at Singleton in the Hunter Valley, NSW; or 2RTB, at Puckapunyal, in central Victoria. Joe was sent to Singleton.

See it from the army's point of view. They had on their hands a bunch of 20-year-old Australian men, some of whom, at least, harboured a resentment or bewilderment at their current predicament. If they were typical of Australian blokes at the time, almost none of them had given any thought to the Defence Force as a career after their school lives. They had other plans and dreams, which most had already begun to live. They were in trades, or in retail, in banks and offices, on the land (a few of them), or in transport, or working as labourers, or working for federal, state, or local government. Many of them had girlfriends, almost all of them had mates, and most of them enjoyed the lives they were fashioning for themselves. A high proportion of them still lived at home with their mums and dads and younger brothers and sisters, and, often enough, mum did most of the work around the house. Cooked, cleaned, maybe even made the beds.

The army had ten weeks to change minds and behaviours. These blokes had to learn to look after themselves. They had to learn to make their own beds the army way, and keep everything around them neat, tidy, clean, and safe. They had to learn to share what was going, to work on common tasks as members of a team, to surrender privacy, and to give up the organisation of their own lives, such as when to take time off, where to go, and with whom. They had to learn how to wear a uniform, how to show proper respect to their betters — and everyone in their new home was more senior, more trained, and therefore superior in every sense to these raw young men. The new recruits learned, right at the very beginning, that they were the lowest of the low, a form of life barely tolerated by all other members of the Australian army. And they had to learn to march.

All this needed to be achieved within the first ten weeks of basic training, and then the instructors would start all over again with the next bunch of new blokes. Those who passed out of basic training had then to be able to learn the harder tasks of infantry, engineering, signals, or whatever, but they could learn nothing if they were not thoroughly Army in all their actions, instincts, and thoughts by the time they left basic training. Basic training, they called it, but it was meant to be mind-altering and behaviour-modifying. Graduates from basic training had to be fitter, tougher, more loyal, and keen on their new life. In ten weeks, they had to become, in a word, soldiers.

It was a big ask, but armies had been doing it for a very long time. Armies all around the world had perfected the techniques required to turn boys into soldiers. In the Australian context, those designing the basic training knew that challenges worked in their favour, that mateship — group loyalty, call it what you will — worked for them. And that fear was not a bad motivator, either — fear of authority, fear of failure, fear of letting your mates down. The first ten weeks were likely to be very rocky. But, almost universally, the army won.

Parents and brothers and sisters flocked to the recruit training centres to witness the 'march out' ten weeks after they had farewelled their son or brother at Swan Street Depot in Melbourne, Victoria Barracks in Sydney, or elsewhere around the country. 'March out' (or 'passing out') was a term the army used that suggested graduation. It marked an achievement, the end of the first step in this new life and the start of the next step, the beginning of corps training. Family members attending the parade didn't know what to expect, and they were usually astonished by what they saw. Onto the parade ground would march a bunch of guys in the uniform of the Australian army, upright in their bearing, proud in their slouch hats. They marched like professional soldiers, as if they had been doing it all their lives; they obeyed every order with snap and precision. They were now soldiers. Those in the stands who were old soldiers might have recognised a few mistakes, but everyone else was gobsmacked with what their sons and brothers had become.

Off the parade ground, hints of the boy of ten weeks ago could still be found. But the lad seemed different, harder perhaps, less interested in Mum and Dad and the kids, more on the lookout for his mates, knowing that he had done things, achieved things that he could not have imagined ten weeks earlier. Already this boy was a changed man, and there were many other changes still to come. How had the army managed that? At the march-out parade, some bloke had droned on about values, mateship, the importance of the uniform, the legacy of the Australian story in earlier times of war and peace. But it wasn't talking that had turned these boys into men. It was something much tougher and more fundamental. Something the new soldiers could not possibly share with their families.

I can't tell you much about Joe's own initial induction into the army; he didn't speak about it at the time with his family, and could never talk about it later. I can tell you one thing, at least: throughout his life, Joe was very proud of his regiment, 5RAR — with a tiger as its mascot — and was always very conscious of once having been a soldier.

He had a few memories of his time in the army that he clung to, but, overwhelmingly, he projected a sense of pride at having worn the uniform, of having been a soldier in a slouch hat. From that, I have always believed that Joe bonded deeply with the army, and had the love and affection of his mates, which he returned.

I would like to be able to tell you of the shock of the new on his first day as he was barked at endlessly for the first time in his life. I would like to be able to tell you of the physical effort, the tiredness, the anxiety of those first weeks, but I cannot. I can tell you, though, that Joe survived, and marched out with all the others, to his own deep satisfaction and joy. But I can't give the actual process of basic training in Joe's own words.

I looked at other accounts of basic training, and, if there is one thing about Australia and the war in Vietnam, it is that it produced some very good writing. One of the best loved of the recent books is Barry Heard's masterly *Well Done, Those Men*. It is a detailed book, relying on a remarkably fresh memory, vivid in its recollections and insights. It's a tragic book, too, because it deals with the horror of post-traumatic stress disorder. Indeed, when I finished it, I thought perhaps Joe wasn't as badly off as I had always believed; at least he had never had PTSD. Yet Heard's book begins with a heavy strain of black humour in a chapter entitled 'Recruit Training, Puckapunyal 1966'.

From the moment the lads stepped off the bus at 'Pucka', as it is always known, they were in strife. They were picked on, victimised, shouted at, deliberately confused, belittled, and addressed in appallingly, shockingly vile language. Their own corporal, 'Corporal Nostrils', originally from South Africa, screamed at them in a version of English they barely understood. Within minutes of their arrival, Corporal Nostrils had the 16 members of his platoon outside their hut and proficient in numbering off 'from the left'. Ten minutes after that, he had them able to turn right as a unit. Small advances, you might think, but actually quite significant in that he had established authority and fear, he had shown that they would be learning everything anew and from the bottom, he had shown them that he was only interested in them as a group, that he had stripped away their individuality and was only interested in one outcome, and that they would learn to do whatever he told them. The other lesson the platoon learned on day one was that a mistake was not worn by the individual, but by the group, and that, therefore, it was in everybody's best interests to help one another and to work together.

For the next ten weeks, the screaming and the shouting and the awful language never ceased. They could be roused out of bed at 10.30 in the night (lights out was at 10.00 p.m.) and then called out again every half hour through the night until they could barely stand up. They became fitter with a punishing physical-fitness program. An officer on hut inspection could put them all on punishment because, although he could not find a speck of dust on his white gloves on their beds and cupboards and window-sills and floors, he did, in triumph, find dust on the roof side of the fluorescent tube of one of the lights.

You might, like me, laugh out loud at Barry Heard's account of the insanity of it all, the pettiness, the sheer awfulness. His version of basic training is simply horrifying. But it was the universal method the army employed to turn boys into soldiers in the early years of this period of conscription. This is precisely what Joe would have experienced even though he was a few hundred kilometres north of Pucka. It was army doctrine and, remarkably, it worked.

For as Heard concludes his brutal account:

> Most of us had changed a great deal. We had survived an abusive training regime that fundamentally assumed we were sub-human, knew nothing, had no skills, and required a frightening, intensive,

> robotic training in the army's ways. I always felt threatened. It could be argued that we had fewer privileges than a modern-day prisoner … Now we all had the same level of fitness, and worked as a team, and support for each other was paramount. It took only one sharp command and we could be out the front of the hut, in the correct uniform, in seconds. I rarely thought of home. There was no time to socialise, and sleep was a precious commodity.

The ten weeks had been gruelling and awful. And yet, there had been profound change:

> It was weird, but as I marched around the parade ground [on the march-out parade] I couldn't recall feeling a prouder moment in my life. We were told we looked good in uniform before the parade, and then in part of the address by the reviewing officer we were told to be proud of the uniform. We had a duty to uphold: we were now part of a tradition, and an honourable one at that. None of it made a lot of sense, but I felt swollen with pride. We were called men … I held my head high, and looked straight ahead with an air of success as I marched off the Puckapunyal parade ground …

After the march-out parade at Singleton, Joe went home to Bell Crescent for a bit of a break — leave that was richly deserved. He came home wearing his uniform, possibly straight off the parade ground. He was proud of his slouch hat, such an identifiable part of Australia's military tradition. His Aunty Gina was at Bell Crescent to welcome him home with all the others. She laughed at the chinstrap, possibly never having seen one before. It looked so silly, she told him, as she tried to lift it from under his lip. Joe knew that he was wearing the chinstrap absolutely correctly and had placed it in exactly the right place as had been drummed into him over the last ten weeks. The chinstrap was important and was worn exactly thus. He looked at his aunt in amazement. He was a soldier, his family were all civilians, and he now knew that there was a yawning gap between them.

Letters

WE KNOW MORE ABOUT WAR now than we have ever known in the past. Military history in earlier times was a matter for specialist writers and readers who were thought to be a little odd in pursuing their interest. Military historians then wrote of strategy and tactics, of the operations of the senior commanders, and of the grand sweep of battle. They, and their readers, had little interest in the doings of the common foot soldiers and wrote instead of regiments 'sweeping to the right' or armies manoeuvring on the great plain of the battlefield. The rank-and-file were to be pushed around as need be.

Although Shakespeare found some humour in the common soldier, nevertheless when he writes of Henry V surveying English losses on the battlefield at Agincourt, he has him reading a list of the names of some of those killed: 'Edward the Duke of York, the Earl of Suffolk, Sir Richard Ketly, Davy Gam, esquire'. And then the king states, 'None else of name'. Much of military history adopted the same approach. Unless the soldier was a senior officer or a person of importance, the military historian was not much interested in him. Who else of name?

In recent times, all this has changed, as historians have discovered that individual soldiers could write eloquently about what they saw, what they suffered, what they made of battle, and how they reconstructed it. Books like Michael Caulfield's *The Unknown Anzacs*, to give but one example, tell 'the real stories of our national legend' through 'the rediscovered diaries and letters of the Anzacs who were there'. Military historians are now in a furious hunt for first-hand accounts and intimate glimpses of battles. Those 'without name' at last take centre stage. But to their families, it was the individual soldier who was always at the centre of their concern, although so many family members will now tell you that 'Dad never spoke about his war'.

When Joe Stawyskyj and all his mates were finishing their initial training, they were required to attend a series of lectures and presentations outlining the various options available to them in the army's structure. They might opt to join the Engineer Corps, the Artillery Corps, or the Catering Corps, for instance. Each man made a careful decision based on the best information he might obtain. Then most of them were placed in the Royal Australian Infantry Corps anyway. Joe went into the Infantry Corps, and was posted to 5RAR — the 5th Battalion, part of the Royal Australian Regiment — eventually to volunteer for training as a forward scout. He was placed in A Company, commanded by Major Reg Sutton, with Captain Bill Grassick as second-in-command. There were three other rifle companies in the battalion, each company consisting of about 110–120 men.

Training was intensive and urgent, as these men might soon go to war. And indeed they did. With only a little more than six months of his two-year service remaining for Joe, 5RAR was ordered to Vietnam. It soon became clear, however, that Joe would have less than six months to serve by the time he arrived in Vietnam, an unusual situation, and the army asked if he wanted to extend his term of service to stay with the battalion for its full tour of duty. He point-blank refused to extend his term for even one day more than the two years required of him, but he agreed to go nonetheless. 'He wanted to stay with his mates', one of his commanding officers remembered, 'because he fitted in very comfortably with his mates ... They were all proud of the fact that they were A Company — the first and the best, they thought.'

The battalion was divided into three groups for movement to

Vietnam: advance party, main party, and rear party. The advance party of 145 men left Holsworthy in the evening of 27 January 1969, and, on the bus to the airport, showed that they were 'high from the obvious liquid farewells during the day'. The main party travelled on HMAS *Sydney* and arrived at Nui Dat, the Australian base, on 15 February 1969. The advance and rear parties travelled more easily and in greater comfort on Qantas aircraft. Joe was a member of the rear party, and arrived in Vietnam a couple of weeks after the main party of his mates.

By this time, 5RAR had settled into routine at Nui Dat, and Joe was very much the new kid on the block. He was in a four-man tent with Mick ('Chook') Fowler, the first forward scout in A Company (Joe was second forward scout), Brian ('Burto') Burton, and one other. Soon after he arrived, his tent mates told him that they were off that evening to the 'Dat Do dogs'. Joe dressed himself up to be spick and span for the night out — to discover that his leg was being vigorously pulled.

There are only three letters from Joe in Vietnam to his family in Bell Crescent. The letters remain in their envelopes to this day. The front of the envelope shows an image of Vietnam in map form featuring five places: Saigon, Nui Dat, Vung Tau, and Phan Rang in the south, and Hanoi in the north. Large lettering indicates that this envelope is to travel 'air mail' back to Australia, the two words separated by a boomerang. On the back of the envelope, there's space for the writer to identify himself. On each of the three letters, Joe has written: '2787617 Pte Stawyskyj 2PL A Coy 5RAR'. He was a soldier on active service. Each letter is of two pages only, and the letters are dated 1 March 1969, 9 March 1969, and 15 March 1969, respectively. It would seem that Joe intended to keep his family completely up-to-date with his doings. Little imagination is needed to understand how eagerly the letters were devoured at home. It was an anxious time for his parents and family, but the letters told them not to worry too much.

There's a slightly stilted manner to the writing, as if letter-writing was a novelty for Joe, which it certainly was. The first begins, 'hope this letter finds you all in good health for as it leaves I am fit and well'. He writes that, so far, he has been on two patrols, 'which were very quite [quiet] and nothing much happened'. In the second paragraph of this letter, Joe states that he has bought a 'transistor radio' for $5.75 that would have cost him at least $20 in Australia, and that there are good watches also to be purchased: 'so if any of you want one let me know and I'll get you one'. He has already seen a watch that he thinks his sister might like, 'so I might get it for her'. He warns that they are about to go out on an operation for eight days and he will not be able to write during this time, 'so don't worry' and 'I'll write as soon as I get back'. 'On the brighter side', he concludes, 'we think that we will be leaving S.V.N. [South Vietnam] about the 3rd or the 10th [of July?]' and he should be back home a day after. He finishes, 'lots of love to everyone'.

His mates thought Joe was a good soldier and that he fitted in well in the platoon and the company. Brian Burton remarked that 'I would follow him into battle any day, I had confidence [in him]'. Captain Bill Grassick recalled that, to him, 'Joe was just one of the soldiers'. It no longer mattered whether a man was a regular soldier or a national serviceman, everyone simply got on with the job. Joe liked to be in the background, Bill Grassick said, more likely to listen than to voice an opinion, but was proud to be in A Company, the best in the battalion, and proud of his role as a forward scout, a position of responsibility and some danger.

Every non-commissioned officer in the company was on his second tour in Vietnam, so there was good experience on which the soldiers could draw. Bill Grassick had served in the New Zealand army in Malaya and was therefore also experienced and highly trained. Having come up through the ranks, he had an instinctive feel for the needs and fears of the diggers.

In his second letter home, Joe says he is still in good health, 'though my feet are a bit sore from all the walking we have done over the last few days'. He is very grateful for a parcel the family has sent over: 'it arrived just as we came back from the bush so we might just have a bit of a party tonight so thanks very much again'. 'Our first operation is over,' he reports, 'and we didn't even see any V.C. ... We stayed mainly around Nui Dat and spent most of the time up in the Waverton [Warburton] Mountains, we found two empty enemy camps which we blew up. We spent about four days up in the mountains and patrolled around the mountains and only found a few footprints. So far everything is going well and I hope I don't see any [Viet Cong] for the next eighty three days, because that's all I've got left in this country before I come home and get discharged.'

Captain David Wilkins, adjutant in 5RAR, who kept a personal diary, tells a different story from the one Joe was sending home. The battalion had been transferred to the Warburton Mountains on 2 March for Operation Quintus Thrust. The first day had been quiet, and 'all were eager to get the first kill'. On 3 and 4 March, things became a little hotter. First Platoon A Company ambushed a group of about seven to eight Viet Cong guerrillas and took them prisoner, while, elsewhere, the battalion made contact with the enemy and overnight accounted for 14 of the enemy killed in action.

On 8 March, the day before Joe was writing his second letter home, 5RAR suffered its first casualties. Tenth Platoon D Company, on operations at 0230 hours, entered, unknowingly, an enemy minefield — and, when a young officer stepped on a mine, Republic of Vietnam soldiers, their allies, started firing on the entire platoon, fearing a VC attack. Three members of 5RAR were killed in action and five wounded. Engineers had to create a safe path through the minefield to extract all the Australians, dead, wounded, and survivors. Joe didn't tell his family anything of this, in the long tradition of Australian soldiers' reticence about saying anything much about battlefield experience.

In his second letter, Joe says that he is pleased with the letters his family had sent to him: 'they were great moral[e] boosters'. Tomorrow, the company would leave on another operation: 'we will be going for about six weeks, so the mail you get might not be quite so often', but he would try. The battalion, in fact, was moved to Long Binh, a huge American base, to assist with the defence of access routes to Saigon in anticipation of another major attack associated with the Tet Festival, the annual celebration of the lunar new year. Playfully, Joe concludes this letter with the comment 'if I get the time next time I will try and write in Ukrainian which should be fun', and he tells his mother in a PS: 'don't send biscuits in a parcel; they get crushed'.

In the third letter, Joe announces that he is 'trying very hard to keep away' from 'hard work' and 'so far I have managed not to do too much of it'. They were back out on operations the second day after they had returned to camp from the first operation, so Joe and his mates have been quite busy, but he thinks they can't have been very far from camp at Nui Dat, as the helicopter trip took only about 15 minutes. He is writing the letter 'sitting on top of a bunker which is on top of a hill in Bien Hoa province. The area is called Long Binh.' 'So far,' he writes, 'we have been here about five days and have done two patrols which have been very [quiet] not even a sight of any V.C. We have done two night ambushes which again were uneventful, but this lack of action doesn't worry me at all.' (David Wilkins reported that the battalion's time at Long Binh was 'boring', though a 'reconnaissance in force operation' on 21 March 'really sweated the cobwebs out'.)

There is a village close to the area in which Joe's patrol is camped. The 'noggy' kids, as he calls them, 'trade us beer and soft drink for soap and any spare rations we might have. We are not supposed to trade with them but we sneak away and do it anyway.' He asks after his brother, 'Johnny', at school, and hopes 'he'll be like his elder brother and come top of the class'. He advises that his sister should 'loaf at Uni', and that he'll send her a radio as soon as he can. 'The weather has been pretty hot', he concludes, 'so far we have had two days when it has rained, boy you should have seen everybody rush to put up tents.'

Whether thoughts of patrols, night ambushes, and 'noggy' kids would have worried his parents, we cannot now know, but it's likely that they felt a considerable unease all the time Joe was in Vietnam. Despite his attempts at reassurance and calm, there was too much on the television and in the newspapers at home to make this all sound easy.

There may have been another letter, which has not survived among his papers, though I doubt it. The incident that will forever change his and his family's lives occurs on 27 March 1969, 12 days after the third letter was written. Joe will never write another letter of his own in his life, and will struggle forever after even to sign his name. About 70 days short of his expected and much anticipated return to Australia, Joe will suffer severe wounds that will never heal. He will never lose that ironic, perhaps sardonic, tone that is glimpsed in his letters. Nor will he ever lose his love and concern for his family, his sense of debt to his parents, his sense of oversight of his younger sister and brother. But he will learn to hate Vietnam and his experience there to the deepest recesses of his heart.

Mines

ALL WEAPONS OF WAR have the same ultimate intention: to inflict maximum damage on as many of the enemy as possible while keeping the cost as low as possible and the numbers operating the weapon as few as possible. It's difficult to construct a hierarchy of awfulness of the weapons of war, but, in any such notional hierarchy, landmines would occupy a special place. They are unseen, are easily deployed, rely on chance to trigger them, and may lay dormant for many months or years. They are utterly devastating and can cause appalling injuries. They terrify both soldiers and civilians, who fear that they may have, unwittingly, blundered into a minefield. Mines are so universal in warfare that the word 'minefield' has passed into our general vocabulary to describe any situation that is hazardous, uncontrolled, and random. Any side resorting to the use of mines in warfare must exercise the utmost caution in deploying them for fear of hurting their own soldiers or the many civilians who are not participants in the war.

Stuart Graham, born on the north coast of New South Wales in 1920, served widely in the Second AIF during the Second World War — including in the North African desert, in forces opposing the 'Desert Fox', Erwin Rommel. There, the young officer learned that both sides defended their positions with a barrier of mines (planted so liberally that, until recently, it was still dangerous to walk over the old battlefields around El Alamein for fear of setting off an unexploded mine). Before mounting any attack on enemy forces in the battles around El Alamein, both sides were required to send in the engineers to clear a series of avenues through the minefields so that the troops might proceed safely.

Graham didn't serve in the Korean War, where he would have observed that the doctrine relating to mines had changed. It became apparent in that war that the use of mines, the laying of a minefield, required that the minefield be constantly protected. This was to avoid the danger that your enemy might simply whip into the minefield and steal the mines you had laid. The enemy could then later use the stolen mines against your own forces.

On 1 January 1967, Stuart Graham became commander of the 1st Australian Task Force, Vietnam (1ATF). He was highly regarded in the Australian army as an intelligent and experienced soldier and, for that reason, his appointment was welcomed. Graham quickly formed the view that the Australian government had provided 1ATF with too few troops to do the job required in some measure of safety and security. Therefore, he looked for ways to better protect his troops from the enemy. His mind ranged across his wartime experience, and he remembered the widespread use of mines in the desert in 1942. He could do the same here, he reasoned, with a barrier of mines, an extensive minefield, that would put space between his troops and the enemy opposing them. He ordered the laying of a wide minefield from Dat Do to the coast, a distance of 11 kilometres.

Everyone warned Brigadier Graham of the danger of what it was that he proposed to do. To protect the Australians in Phuoc Tuy province and to deny the enemy access to food and supplies, Graham would construct a minefield containing more than 20,000 mines. Even troops lower down the chain of command thought this was a questionable tactic, for fear of mines was widespread among the soldiers. 'But, sir', people said as they heard of his plan. A minefield must be defended — permanently, constantly, thoroughly. This is core doctrine. It was Graham's idea that the minefield was to be protected by troops from the army of the Republic of Vietnam; but Graham's engineer adviser at headquarters, Major Brian Florence, told the commander that the minefield could not be defended by anyone. 'Sir', others also told him, 'you will simply be supplying ammunition to the enemy.' But Stuart Graham would not listen.

In *The Minefield: an Australian tragedy in Vietnam*, a damning book by an academic and former Australian army officer, Greg Lockhart shows what was at stake. Twenty thousand mines there for the taking. Indeed, the mines were clearly being taken up by the enemy and stored for later use against the Australians even as Graham continued to lay more mines. It was madness.

The enemy became expert in the harvesting and laying of mines. They would treat the Australian minefield with great respect, knowing how very dangerous it was. To extract a mine from the ground was difficult and potentially fatal. The Viet Cong used local village women to do this work. The women would enter the minefield barefooted and use their toes to locate the mines that the Australians had laid. Carefully, they would seek to disable the mine before taking it from the ground. The VC would then place these mines in areas where they expected the Australians to be — and would remove and re-lay them if the Australians didn't pass through an area they had mined. The VC also had access to Chinese mines, which they used against the Australians wherever they could. So the Australians were on high alert whenever they were out in the field, wary and anxious.

Was the laying of this extensive minefield the mistake of one man? A mistake that no one could speak up against as Graham was their commander? This isn't Greg Lockhart's explanation. He shows that Graham wasn't alone. Others around him in Vietnam, and above him back home — in the military and among the politicians — simply had no understanding of the war they had agreed to fight and the enemy that they were fighting. Lockhart, who fought in Vietnam himself, concludes that those in charge were, in fact, fighting the wrong war. Pity help the ordinary soldiers, then, who were sent to fight this 'wrong war'.

Peter Gration — who also served in Vietnam, and who rose in rank and position to become Chief of Army and then, for long years, Chief of the Defence Force — agreed with Lockhart. Launching a book in 1987 at the Australian War Memorial, Gration said, 'the truth is that we knew very little about the province when we went in — of its long history of struggle against the French, of its history as a Viet Minh stronghold in the war against the French … of the almost complete control of the province by the VC in 1966 based on a strongly entrenched political and military organisation and extensive popular support'. Knowing little, the Australians should have been cautious and wary. But here was Brigadier Graham blundering in, overriding his subordinates, refusing to listen to their sensible advice, and laying a minefield such as he had known in the North African desert in 1942.

The consequences were tragic. An Australian minefield, taken up by the enemy and used against the Australians. Hundreds of mines, more likely thousands of mines — as if Graham had opened a supermarket for his enemy, stocking only mines, all of them free of charge to the procurer, except for the casualties involved in taking them from the shelves. The VC use of these mines against their Australian enemies caused, Greg Lockhart estimates, at least 50 per cent of all Australian casualties in 1969 and 1970, spiking, he calmly tells us, to 80 per cent of Australian casualties at some points.

Landmines and anti-personnel mines are evil weapons, rightly feared by all Australian soldiers on operations. That some of those that injured Australian soldiers in Vietnam were Australian in origin was a terrible indictment of those making the decisions in this war. Far too many of those Australians killed and maimed in Vietnam were cruelly and shockingly injured by our own actions. When we turn to an examination of the events that caused Joe Stawyskyj his terrible wounds, and his lifelong retreat into care and a wheelchair, we should remember that the mines that were deployed by both sides were at the heart of his tragedy.

Tragedy

COLIN KHAN WAS COMMANDER of 5RAR from 27 November 1967 until 30 June 1970. With the rank of lieutenant-colonel, Khan took the battalion to Vietnam in 1969. Naturally, he was known to the men as 'Genghis'. It was his responsibility to ensure that the Commanders Diary Narrative was completed each day, to give an explanation of the battalion's activities that day. Like all the others from this war, the Commanders Diary Narrative is spare, succinct, administrative, unemotional, and full of acronyms. You need to be a specialist military historian to unearth much of the information it may contain. It's a paradox, because Lieutenant-Colonel Khan was a well-loved commander then and a much loved figure in the continuing life of the battalion now. He took a close interest in the welfare of his men 'in country', but you would never know that from looking at the Narrative. An army is an impersonal bureaucracy, among other things.

On 27 March 1969 at 0729 (now isn't that precise), the battalion began moving from Area of Operations Arunda to Area of Operations Manuka, though only specialists need to be concerned about the precise location of these places. The rumours that the enemy were to launch either an all-out attack on Saigon or an attack on Long Binh had proved to be wrong, and 5RAR was going to somewhere of more significance. David Wilkins, the adjutant, observed that the move was proving to be a 'complete monster', as the battalion was taking so much gear with it. Battalion Headquarters and C Company were moved by armoured personnel carriers, B Company flew in helicopters to an area of ground now secured by the recently arrived C Company, and A Company moved by road along Route 1 into the south-west portion of Area of Operations Manuka. D Company remained in Area of Operations Arunda for the time being.

So far, all was routine, though there was a world of difference between the transport options chosen for the three companies on the move. C Company was inside (relatively) secure armour; B Company, taking to the skies, was perhaps the company most safely transported. Luck of the draw, A Company was accommodated in so-called Troop Carrying Vehicles, on loan from the Americans. There were four of these trucks, with large open trays behind the driver's cabin. Most of the soldiers were seated on fold-down seats running down both sides of each truck's tray, though some remember that Joe Stawyskyj and perhaps a few others were standing. The soldiers' packs and equipment had been piled into the centre of the tray, and Joe had braced himself against this. Putting it at its simplest, the men in A Company were travelling by a much less secure method than their mates. They were vulnerable.

The Commanders Diary Narrative now concentrates on A Company only. At 1015, two of the trucks struck landmines, placed 50 metres apart. It 'appeared that mines were pressured detonated'; that is, they were not operated by enemy troops in the area. The two trucks were badly damaged and 22 men were wounded; only ten remained on duty. That's over two-thirds casualties — these are shocking proportions and indicate the savagery of the attack. Ten Australians, two United States servicemen, and one South Vietnamese soldier were evacuated immediately.

The Commanders Diary Narrative now turns to other matters on that same day. At 1112, elements of the battalion, on patrol, discovered rifle pits and a command post that had not been used for some time. After a further search, the patrol uncovered even more pits, documents, ammunition, and medical supplies. So Area of Operations Manuka had well merited the attention of 5RAR. The work of the battalion went on, relentlessly, despite the tragedy to A Company. The Narrative goes on relentlessly, too, day after day, telling of troop movements and patrols, of contact with the enemy, of search-and-destroy operations, indicative of the tedium, excitement, danger, and sheer hard work of an infantry soldier in a war as difficult as that in Vietnam.

Colin Khan's war diary has given us the outline of what happened to A Company as it moved to its new area of responsibility and effort. There is much more that can be said of the human dimensions of what happened to the Australian and other soldiers that morning in late March. Bill Grassick, second-in-command of A Company, 5RAR, takes up the story. Grassick was an experienced officer. He had joined the New Zealand army, against his parents' wishes, at 16 years of age and had served in that army for 11 and a half years. He had then joined the Australian army in 1967. Grassick had served with New Zealand in the Malayan Emergency: 'I was always very comfortable in the jungle.' He found his service in Vietnam 'much more intense ... It was certainly a lot more dangerous ... the Viet Cong were very, very expert at placing mines in the most unusual places.'

Bill Grassick has written a graphic account of what happened to A Company on 27 March. 5RAR had been given the job of securing the approach route to Long Binh (this was Area of Operations Manuka), to clear the road and its surrounds of an enemy that was making travel along the route dangerous and unpredictable. To assist in the operation, 5RAR had been given additional weapons and ammunition beyond what could be carried by '2 legged mules', as Bill Grassick put it. So the trucks were called in to transport the men and their extra equipment. But there were more men than the trucks could carry, so one platoon of A Company and a part of Company Headquarters were placed in the much safer armoured personnel carriers (APCs).

It's important in the story that the APCs accompanied the trucks. It seems that the Viet Cong were present along the road in some force, anticipating the movement of the Australian troops. However, when they saw the heavily armed APCs accompanying the more-exposed trucks, the VC withdrew rather than remaining to ambush the survivors of the expected mine attack. What was a tragedy might well have been a disaster for all of A Company without the presence of the APCs.

Bill Grassick admitted that he was apprehensive about riding in the cabin of one of the trucks, which would follow one of the APCs. An American sergeant had told him that the Americans didn't know the route they were taking and, if the trucks lost contact with the APCs, there should be an Australian officer in the convoy who knew the way and could direct them to their destination. Grassick had reluctantly agreed to climb into the cabin of the first truck, rationalising that, as they were on a sealed road, there could be little danger from mines.

It was a hot day, Grassick recalled, and he was soon drifting off to sleep. Occasionally, he would open his eyes to check on the APC in front of him. Looking up some time into the journey, Grassick discovered to his great surprise and alarm that the convoy had turned off the sealed road and was now travelling on a dirt road and that the APCs were charging on ahead. He didn't know why the route had changed and he was uncomfortable with the change. He couldn't get to his radio, because the radio and its operator were on the tray of the truck, behind and above him. Was it as simple as somebody deciding to take a short cut? If this was the case then it seems highly unmilitary and, we might think, irresponsible. Has the reason for the route diversion ever been explained? It was dangerous that Grassick was unable to make radio contact with the APCs and his superior officer, Reg Sutton. You might say that the convoy was now out of control.

Grassick's alarm increased considerably when he observed an old Vietnamese peasant woman on the side of the road on which they were travelling. She would have known the area well — it was her place, her village, perhaps she even had a small bit of land. She knew the people of the village and the area, the farmers, the traders, the kids, and the VC. She knew their business as well as she knew her own. As the truck that was carrying Bill Grassick and his Australian soldiers passed by, this woman squatting by the side of the road was shaking her head, as if to say, 'Don't go there; it is too dangerous; keep out — land mines ahead.' Another soldier on the trucks that day, Brian Burton, who shared a tent with Joe, also saw the woman by the side of the road. He remembers that she drew her thumb across her throat, in an even clearer indication of the danger into which the Australians had stumbled.

Thoroughly alert now, Grassick told his driver to put the truck's wheels into precisely the same tracks that had been made by the APC in front of them. The driver's response was almost as chilling as the sight of the old woman warning them of danger: he told Grassick that the APC tracks were wider than the truck's wheelbase and he asked which track he should steer into. Grassick told him to pick the best-looking one, but, as he said this, he realised that this seemingly routine movement of troops had gone hopelessly wrong. These men were already in considerable danger.

Bill Grassick was in the lead truck; by luck of the draw — again — Joe Stawyskyj was in the second truck. Joe's good mate of later years Sigmund ('Siggy') Jablonski was standing on the tray of the third truck, right behind Joe's, and he takes up the story. Suddenly there was an enormous explosion. Noise, dust, terror, and uncertainty. So much dust, indeed, that it seemed almost like night-time. The second truck had struck a landmine. Observers could never understand why the first truck had passed through clear and Joe's truck had been blown up. Some have learned to call this 'survivor guilt'. Why did I survive when better men than me took a whack? Bill Grassick's American driver screamed 'Ambush!' as he heard the sound of the first explosion, and immediately accelerated. 'He panicked', said Bill Grassick simply. Grassick shouted at him to stop so that they could assist the wounded behind them. And then, as he put it, 'the sun went out'.

Bill Grassick had heard nothing, but there was dust everywhere, 'intense dust', he called it, and things seemed now to be moving in slow motion. Grassick was lifted from his seat — he could feel that — and his rifle was tumbling away from him. He seemed to think that the slow motion was so slow that he could even see specks of dust swirling all about. Then real time returned with an immense thud as the truck fell back to earth 'minus much of the front of it'. So Grassick's truck had hit a mine, too, but the damage was less severe. Both trucks had struck mines, the first after the second. There was dust and debris everywhere and overwhelming confusion.

Then training and long experienced kicked in. The training was to immediately disembark the vehicle. Siggy Jablonski recalls diving off his truck within seconds of the first blast, almost by instinct. Instinctively, too, the soldiers would have gone to the side of the road to set up defensive positions in case of a further attack, from an armed enemy witnessing the confusion and chaos. Fearing that anti-personnel mines might have been deployed by the side of the road, Grassick yelled at his men to use the vehicles as cover and not to take cover in the roadside ditches. Grassick agrees that, in all the din and danger, few of his soldiers would have heard his shouted commands. Following the noise of the explosions, no one could hear anything much at all; he himself would be deaf in his left ear for at least two weeks. Nevertheless, while medics rushed to the wounded Australians, the rest of his men gathered around or even under the vehicles. The clarity of Bill Grassick's thinking and his overriding concern for the safety and security of his men is striking and deeply impressive.

Using frantic sign language, Grassick managed to regroup his troops and set up some sort of defensive perimeter. His driver had suffered severe damage to his legs and was screaming in pain. The shock of the situation was profound — wounded men with awful injuries, the expectation of a major attack from an unseen enemy, and a huge crater in the middle of the road indicating the force of the explosion.

The company medic, Dave Christensen, began attending to the casualties, of whom about a dozen needed immediate medical evacuation. He discovered that Joe Stawyskyj was in real strife, unconscious and unmoving since he had landed on the road. Dave got him into a semi-prone position before attending the other wounded soldiers. They were being treated now with morphine to ease the frightful pain, but they were in urgent need of specialist medical help. The radio operator could just make contact with the base at Nui Dat, asking for 'Dust-off'. Within minutes, it seemed, helicopters arrived, and, with great skill, the American pilots landed as close as they could to the scene of the mayhem.

Joe Stawyskyj appeared to be the most severely wounded of the Australians. Indeed, many of his mates thought he had been killed. He had been standing on the tray of the second truck. Did he understand how much danger he was in as the convoy took to the dirt road? Probably not. Was he carrying on with his mates, as soldiers do, joking and talking, in this downtime from hard work? Probably. What is almost certain is that Joe had no time to prepare himself for what was about to happen. No time to brace, no time to grab at anything to protect himself. Soldiers remembered seeing him travelling through the air in an arc from the truck before hitting the ground on his head.

The first vehicle struck the mine with its front wheels, which meant that the engine block took most of the force of the mine, protecting those on the tray of the truck, and the occupants of the cabin, to an extent. The rear wheels of the second vehicle struck its mine, which meant that the tray on which the soldiers were riding took the brunt of the blast. Soldiers later agreed that it was lucky they were travelling on American trucks, made of steel, rather than the more flimsy Australian vehicles. It was entirely fortuitous what happened next, not unlike when a shell lobbed into a trench on the Western Front. One soldier, standing next to his mate, might die instantly from the impact of the blast; another, a few feet along the trench, might survive, almost unscathed — in body, anyway. Joe was hurled up in the air and pitched backwards along the road. Landing on his head caused him severe trauma. He was rendered unconscious, of course, and it would be many months before he regained consciousness. Both his ankles were fractured from the impact of the blast, and his feet severely wounded. There was also damage to his face and mouth.

Later that day, his mates tried to find out what had become of him after the helicopter carrying him lifted off. They searched the Australian army medical system, hoping for news that he was alright. It took some time to find out where he was. Because the casualties were rescued by Americans, they were taken to the nearest American hospital, the American 93rd Field Hospital, where Joe could receive immediate attention. When, eventually, he was returned to the Australian army medical system, it was discovered that those who had worked so intensely on Joe's head, the site of the major trauma, had missed the obvious and significant damage to his ankles and feet. Joe would never again walk steadily. Never walk, in fact, more than a few yards, and those with assistance, for the remainder of his life. From this moment on, Joe would be bound to a wheelchair for all his waking hours, relying on it for any movement whatsoever.

Bill Grassick, though hurt in the assault, was not hospitalised, and continued his duties. About six weeks later, though, he and almost 60 of his soldiers came across a 400-strong enemy unit and engaged in a brief but intense firefight. One soldier was killed and 38 wounded, including himself. These were, again, appalling proportions. Bill spent seven months in hospital, at one stage fearing that he would lose a leg, but he recovered from his wounds to continue his career in the army. He retired in 1991. He claims, with some pride and considerable regret, that 5RAR in this yearlong tour of duty suffered the greatest number of casualties of any Australian battalion in the Vietnam war — 28 killed and 247 wounded.

Bill Grassick's account of this tragedy to A Company, 5RAR, concludes on an awful note. 'Sometime after the immediate crisis,' he wrote, 'a Thai cavalry unit turned up to assist'. Grassick talked to the Thai officer in charge of the unit, who said that he was amazed that the Australians had turned onto this road with wheeled vehicles. The Thai headquarters had already advised the Australian Task Force Headquarters, repeatedly, that the road was heavily mined and should be avoided. Later, Grassick asked an Australian staff officer at the 1ATF HQ if this were so. The officer admitted that the Thais had passed the information on to the Australians, who had not passed it down the line, as they did not believe it to be true. The incident might have been averted if those on the operation had been given the fullest information available. And Joe might have finished his tour of duty in Vietnam in good health and with eager expectations for the future.

On the Steps of the Memorial

SATURDAY 3 OCTOBER 1992 was a great day for every returned man and woman who had served in Vietnam. In Canberra on that day, the governor-general, Bill Hayden, unveiled or inaugurated (according to your pleasure) the Australian Vietnam Forces National Memorial on Anzac Parade, joining the other memorials on the parade (to the Army, to the Light Horse, to the Royal Australian Air Force, and to many others). It was reported that fully one half of all Australian Vietnam veterans still living marched down Anzac Parade that morning. Joe Stawyskyj was one of them, although his 'marching' was done from his wheelchair.

The veterans had reason to be proud of their achievement in creating this memorial, even though some of them wondered about its enclosed nature. It is not a traditional memorial. The veterans had raised most of the money required to build the memorial themselves; they had created an executive body to manage its development, and had also created an assessor panel to judge the various proposals for the memorial. They had spent $1.2 million on its erection, towards which the federal government contributed a mere $250,000 and the land on which the memorial stood (already permanently reserved for memorials along Anzac Parade). Those were meaner times then for veterans. The memorial had been a very long time in coming, opened 17 years after the last serviceman had left Vietnam. The main feature of the ceremony was the march down Anzac Parade of thousands of those who had served in Vietnam, with the governor-general taking the salute. There were wreaths and speeches and remembrance, but the veterans from the war had pride of place.

At the top of Anzac Parade stands the Australian War Memorial, one of the most important and best-loved buildings in Canberra, and of which I was then the deputy director. As an institution, we were not involved in the vast ceremony on 3 October. Many Australians think the War Memorial somehow controls the other memorials in its vicinity, but, in reality, the War Memorial has nothing to do with their approval, siting, design, or maintenance. However, senior management at the Memorial wanted to do something to mark this great occasion. For some time, Vietnam veterans had felt that they were somehow 'poor cousins' at the Memorial in terms of exhibition space and the retelling of their story; they believed that they were somehow looked down on in comparison to veterans from the earlier wars — and we were keen to dispel this view and to be as welcoming as possible.

So it was decided to hold a special commemorative service at the Australian War Memorial in the evening of the preceding day, Friday 2 October, for the immediate families of the 500 or so Australians who had lost their lives in Vietnam. It would be a simple ceremony, to be held in the Memorial's noble Commemorative Courtyard, surrounded by the bronze tablets of the national Roll of Honour, listing the names of all Australian dead from all wars in which Australia had been involved. The courtyard — with the Roll of Honour, the Pool of Reflection, the Eternal Flame, and the great Hall of Memory at its far end — gives a sense of awe even to the most casual visitor. The courtyard speaks of sadness and mourning for all those who lost their lives, and hope that they had not died in vain. Though the Hall of Memory did not yet contain the Tomb of the Unknown Australian Soldier (which brought to the whole place a new sense of meaning), nevertheless, the Australian War Memorial's courtyard had long been seen as Australia's most important place of remembrance.

It wasn't easy to find the names of all of the next of kin of those who had been killed in Vietnam, and, although the War Memorial advertised its service as widely as funds would allow, it is probable that the families of some of the war dead didn't know of the ceremony or couldn't afford to attend it. Even so, organisers at the Memorial anticipated a high level of participation, and they were not disappointed. The ceremony was held in the early evening, after the Memorial had closed to its normal visitors for the day — and, as soon as the great bronze gates swung open for the second time that day, a reverent and largely silent crowd began to assemble in the Commemorative Courtyard.

From the first moments of that remarkable early-spring evening, it was apparent that we had done something of significance for those whose overwhelming emotion the next day would be of sadness. As the veterans the next day marched in their mass numbers down Anzac Parade, a small portion of the crowd would be only too aware that their loved one was not there in the march. Words would be said recalling their loss, but the starkness of that loss, the awful inequality between the living and the dead, would be forced on these grieving families. It was this sense that the War Memorial's ceremony was designed to address.

Michael had driven Joe down to Canberra for the Vietnam Forces National Memorial opening. Joe was as keen as could be to march in the parade with his mates, and to enjoy their company after. For him, it would be like a second Anzac Day in the one year — Anzac Day each year being for Joe, most certainly, the 'one day of the year' when he was among those with whom he served, all of them glad that he was there, sharing even in his disabled state a sense of friendship and common experience, almost as if they were all family. It would be like that again on this special day, Joe was sure of that. Using my privileged position as one of the three most senior people at the War Memorial,

I had suggested to the director that I might bring my father-in-law to our ceremony, though, of course, his son still lived. No one at the Memorial saw this as inappropriate, and Michael, though shy as ever, had agreed to come along.

The sole focus of the ceremony, simple and brief, though intensely moving, was on all those who had been killed in Vietnam. Their names were behind us, at the far end of the Roll of Honour, so much smaller than the Roll for either the First or Second world wars, but no less honoured for that. The ceremony started with a brief word of welcome from the Australian War Memorial Council's chairman (her legislatively decreed title), Dame Beryl Beaurepaire, who, as usual, spoke simply, honestly, and, most importantly, in the voice of a woman who had served, who had experienced loss of life in war, and, though she did not explicitly draw on this, who was a mother. There were hymns, with the assistance of the Royal Military College, and words from the national president of the RSL and an army chaplain.

Three wreaths were laid: the first by the acting chief of the Defence Force, Vice-Admiral Ian MacDougall, the second by the minister for veterans' affairs, Ben Humphreys, and the third by a young woman, 22-year-old Lisa Hardy, representing all the next-of-kin. She had been born after her father's death in Vietnam, and, because her mother wasn't married to her father, two years passed before mother and daughter learned that their special soldier had been killed. A week before the ceremony in Canberra, Lisa discovered that she had a grandfather, and they had met for the first time at the War Memorial that day.

To conclude the ceremony after the wreath-laying, the Last Post was played from the bridge above the courtyard, at the far end, reverberating powerfully around the enclosed, sacred space. There was a minute of silence, and the silence was overpowering, and then the Reveille. The ceremony was at an end.

A silent and deeply emotional crowd began to move to the single exit from the courtyard, through the main gates of the Memorial, and then down the stairs. No one spoke. Many were in tears. The sense of loss all these years later was still palpable. I suggested that Michael stand back to let the crowd dissipate, for he was an old man now, and I did not want him to feel anxious in the crush. It was obvious to me that he, too, had been deeply moved by the ceremony, and might even have been somewhat shocked or overawed by it. It might have been the first such ceremony Michael had ever attended, because Joe always went to the Anzac Day march with his mates, never with his parents.

By now, Michael and I were almost alone in the courtyard, and I indicated to him that it was time to leave. We walked down the stairs from the Roll of Honour gallery and into the Commemorative Courtyard itself, passing the Stone of Remembrance, which was festooned with the wreaths that had been laid during the ceremony, wreaths which reminded us again of death and loss. Coming to the Memorial's gates, which officials were about to shut, we paused at the top of the stairs to look down Anzac Parade, where the great ceremony would be held tomorrow. Michael looked down the parade and then looked at me. In a soft voice, with deep emotion, he said, 'He should have died, Joe, he should have died.' It was the saddest thing anyone had ever said to me.

Hearing the News

MOST OF JOE'S MATES with him on that day on that dusty road in Vietnam, in the immediate chaos after the detonation of the mines, believed that Joe would die. Joe was obviously unconscious, immobile, and with terrible wounds to his body. No one with him believed that he could survive; most thought him already dead. And there was so much to do, creating the defensive perimeter and preparing for the expected attack from enemy forces. Swiftly evacuated by chopper to an American hospital, Joe was lost to his mates, who were rightly concerned for their own survival as they remained in a defensive position while their rescue was organised. That night, they remembered Joe briefly, but without too much emotion, for soldiers can't allow themselves that. They spared a thought for his bereft parents and his family.

Michalina had begun the second year of her university studies just a few weeks earlier and was at home alone on Friday 28 March. It was about three o'clock in the afternoon. Michalina's parents were at work, her younger brother, John, was at his primary school, and she was organising herself for the coming year and perhaps even doing a little studying or reading. She had a full program of work for the year ahead.

Michalina was in the front room, she remembers, the living room, when she saw a car pull up outside the house in Bell Crescent. This in itself was unusual, as few cars came down Bell Crescent, apart from residents' cars, and very few cars ever stopped outside her house. She looked carefully to see what was going on, and saw a man in army uniform emerge from the car. 'This can't be good', she remembers thinking to herself.

Opening the front door, she heard the officer say that he had a telegram to deliver to Michael Stawyskyj, and was he in? Michalina explained that he was at work at the Borg-Warner factory, a few minutes' drive away, and together they drove to the factory to find her father. The officer gave the telegram to Michael and offered to drive on to Anna's workplace and then take them all home. Fearing the worst, Michael left the telegram unopened, to share the moment of discovery with his wife. Within a few further minutes, Anna had been collected and they were all back at home, to read the telegram alone, together now in their grief. The army officer had left them, his duty done.

An earlier telegram from AustForce Vietnam had been received by a variety of official recipients in Canberra and Melbourne probably shortly after midday on 27 March, given the time difference between Nui Dat and Canberra. The telegram placed the action in Bien Hoa province and gave a precise grid reference. It stated that injuries had been received by '2787617 pte j stawyskyj' when 'tcv [Troop Carrying Vehicle] struck mine on road'. It gave the condition of the soldier as 'very seriously ill' and stated that he had received 'closed head wound, fractured left and right ankles, fractured right thumb'. It also stated 'nok [next of kin] not advised'. In other words, it would be the responsibility of the army in Australia to let the next of kin know.

The telegram that Michael and Anna opened the next day read: 'it is learned with regret that your son 2787617 private jarslow stawyskyj was placed on the very seriously ill list on 27 march 1969 at 24 evacuation hospital long binh vietnam as a result of injuries sustained in action in bien hoa province vietnam. a progress report will be forwarded to you at regular intervals but if a change of condition occurs you will be notified immediately. army headquarters'. At once, said Gina, Anna looked like an old lady. 'It was very hard with the news', said Gina, and Anna couldn't stop crying.

But what was the news and how could these people interpret it? The telegram merely said that Joe was 'very seriously ill' as a result of action. Had he been shot, blown up, were there broken bones, vicious wounds, was he to be operated on, what was the chance of recovery, or were they merely waiting and expecting him to die, with an immediate notification to the grieving family? No one was saying what had happened, nor could the family know what to expect. Nor was there anything to do. They couldn't rush to Joe's bedside, they couldn't talk earnestly with the doctors about the likely progress of the patient, they couldn't bring in the priest for Joe's final sacrament — they could do nothing but wait and hope and pray.

The newspapers in the weeks before 27 March 1969 showed the family that, for Australian troops, service in Vietnam was, at best, unpredictable. No Australian soldier was killed in January 1969. For the first two weeks of February, there were only two reports of Australian soldiers dying; both died from wounds received months before. On 17 February, it was reported that one Australian soldier had been killed in action and two were wounded in battle. And on 18 February, it was reported that two Australian soldiers had been killed and eight wounded in battle. The rest of the month was reasonably quiet, giving some hope to those at home eagerly scanning the newspapers. But Joe was at war, and that was and must be inherently dangerous, so the telegram when it came was the culmination of a constant anxiety that those at home had experienced.

The newspapers also gave some indication of what had happened to Joe beyond the appallingly indifferent official casualty telegram. Australian newspapers reported on Saturday 29 March 1969 that 'three Australian soldiers, including one national serviceman, were injured in action in Bien Hoa province when enemy mines damaged two troop carrying vehicles ... all of the wounded are members of the 5th Battalion, Royal Australian Regiment ... one of them Private Jarslow Stawyskyj, national serviceman, 22, single, of Fairfield, NSW, is in a very serious condition'. So that was it: it was a mine. The other two soldiers injured in the action 'are in a very satisfactory condition.' So that is good; perhaps Joe will soon join them on the 'satisfactory' list and pull through. A glimmer of hope.

How could life go on over the next few days? There was absolutely nothing that the family could do except wait for further news. Of course, there were prayers at the Ukrainian Catholic church at Lidcombe; friends would come to offer support and kindness, bringing food, trying to find some way of helping. But these kind people asked questions — what happened, how bad is he, what is being done for him, will he come home, when will he recover, how long — and there were no answers to any of these questions. Michael, Anna, Michalina, and John, Gina, John, Lida, Bobbie, and little Stephen waited in an agony. Stephen loved his Aunty Anna dearly, yet all he saw was that she was forever crying and he really didn't know why. Australians observed Easter Sunday on 6 April in 1969, and so there were the holidays to endure. Ukrainian Easter would be a week later, and many in the church at Lidcombe were praying for Joe.

The next telegram among the family records is dated 9 April 1969, and I can find no earlier record in the official file of a telegram to Michael between 28 March and 9 April, so it would seem that this was only the second telegram between army headquarters and the family. All at Bell Crescent had endured the agony of waiting for further news across these 12 days. Twelve days with no news at all. Indifferent and cruel in the extreme. Michalina had to go back to university, John had to go back to school, did Michael go back to work? Probably.

The second telegram, also marked urgent, was delivered at 4.20 p.m. on Wednesday 9 April. It read, 'still very seriously ill but medically evacuated from vietnam to malaysia. advice has now been received that your son 2787617 private jarslow stawyskyj was medically evacuated to 4 royal australian air force hospital butterworth malaysia on 7 april 1969. army headquarters'. But still there was nothing on the nature of Joe's wounds, about his prospects for recovery, or any news about what was being done to make him better, any news about whether he would live or die. The family merely knew that Joe was no longer in a war zone, but whether this was a good thing or a bad thing, they couldn't possibly guess. And so the waiting went on, the nightmare endured.

The third telegram to the next of kin was received on Thursday 17 April at 11.50 a.m. It was brief and, again, completely uninformative: 'still very seriously ill. it is learned with regret that the condition of your son private 2787617 jarslow stawyskyj on 16 april 1969 was still very seriously ill. army headquarters'.

Perhaps people of more sophistication in the ways of Australian society, people who were more accustomed to dealing with public servants and senior military officials, people who knew their way around would by now have been being raising hell with someone to find out something. Or perhaps someone would have approached the local member of parliament or an important friend high up in the law, business, the church, the university. But Michael and Anna knew no one of substance or influence, no one who could take up their cause and find out what was really going on.

But they must have been doing something, asking someone for help, making a little bit of a fuss in their agony of unknowing. On 22 April 1969, Military Command in Sydney sent a telegram to superiors in either Canberra or Melbourne: 'appreciated if further details of condition could be provided to relief stress of parents'. Further details of condition? So far, all that they had been told was that Joe was 'very seriously ill'. Surely — even some in the army were now saying, nearly a month after the tragedy — the family might be told what happened and how Joe was. Yet this advice was evidently ignored. On Wednesday 23 April, Michael received a fourth telegram: 'it is learned with regret that the condition of your son 2787617 private jarslow stawyskyj on 23 april 1969 was still very seriously ill. army headquarters'.

There was an almost daily telegram between the hospital and Canberra about Joe's condition, which makes his file in the National Archives very thick, but provides no real insight into what was happening. Each day, a telegram came, 'condition unchanged', but there was no need to tell the next of kin this every day. Too much information. Essentially, Joe had gone into a coma at the moment his head crashed into the road and he hadn't yet emerged from the coma, although one telegram suggests that he briefly regained consciousness in Vietnam. There would have been intervention in the hospitals to reduce swelling in his brain, yet what otherwise could the medical staff do but wait? It might have been a kindness, though, to let the parents know.

Canberra knew that Joe would be 'medevaced' to Australia on 6 May 1969, 'with medical officer in attendance', but, again, no one thought to tell the family of this coming transfer. Instead, the next telegram Michael received was on Wednesday 7 May 1969, stating: 'still very seriously ill but medically evacuated to australia. it is learned that your son 2787617 private jarslow stawyskyj returned to australia on 7 may 1969 and is now located at repatriation general hospital concord nsw. army headquarters'. So, finally, Joe's mother and father and sister and little brother might see Joe, see for themselves what 'very seriously ill' actually meant. At long last, his mother, in her grief and intense sadness, might hold Joe's hand, stroke his hair, kiss his face and forehead, and look after and care for her broken boy.

The Repat

REPATRIATION IS THE PROCESS of returning something or someone to the land of origin, and the word derives from the Latin 'patria', meaning 'fatherland', 'native land', 'country'. In Australia, however, usually abbreviated to 'repat', the word came to have two main meanings. It was either the name for the (much unloved) department that handled veterans' and war widows' entitlements, pensions, and welfare from 1917 onwards or a shortening for 'repatriation hospital', the place where veterans were sent for health care.

The repat hospitals were among the few hospitals in Australia owned and managed by the Commonwealth. There was one large repat hospital in each capital city with the exception of Canberra and Darwin. If a man — usually they were men — had to go into the repat, it might involve moving a considerable distance away from home and family.

The repat in Sydney was at Concord, an inner west Sydney suburb, on the edge of the Parramatta River. It was well sited on a peninsula of land, and was surrounded by parks and car parks. Built between 1939 and 1942 as the Yaralla Military Hospital, it was the largest hospital in Australia when it opened, with 2,000 beds. It was also one of the tallest buildings in Sydney at the time, and won a prestigious architectural award. After the Second World War, Concord, as it was always known, no longer gave care to serving soldiers, but became a repatriation hospital for veterans. No members of the general public were treated at the hospital before 1974.

Joe entered Concord on 7 May 1969 and was there until sometime in 1972. He was placed in a general ward, though his bed was always screened by curtains. There were very few, if any, private rooms at Concord at the time. Joe remained in a coma for many months and was fed intravenously. As soon as they were able, possibly on the day he arrived at the repat, the family visited Joe to see for themselves what he was like, the telegrams having been so uninformative. Joe's condition must have given them a terrible shock. In Gina's words, 'for six months he was like a dead body'. It is an exact description of what the family found: a lifeless, immobile body, with no responses to any stimulation whatsoever, with no capacity to communicate, and with no apparent hope of recovery. The doctors simply said that they must wait. Officially, they listed Joe's woes as 'brain injury, bilateral fractured calcanei [both heel bones fractured] and dislocated right ankle joint'.

Though he was in a permanent coma and therefore completely unresponsive — and this is a most extraordinary aspect of Joe's whole story — there was almost always a member of the family with him during these first months at Concord, and for the years thereafter. Anna could not be forever and permanently at his bedside, but she spent long hours there every day. When she was needed at home, Michael, John, or Gina took over the watch. Because of their differing hours of work on shifts, they were able to arrange this. Of course, when the hospital closed to visitors, they could not be present, but, during visiting hours, there was almost always someone with Joe. Michalina and John couldn't be present during the day, as one was at university and the other at school, but, after the evening meal, every day, both parents and both siblings set off for Concord to be with Joe.

Every day. Month after month. Across the years. Watching for any sign that Joe might return to life. Telling him of what their day had been like for them, of their work, study, news of the day; talking to him as if he could understand. His parents had determined that Joe, their oldest child, their elder son, was their responsibility, that they must care for him as best they possibly could. We read of parents who put their lives on hold for a child when it is sick, say with cancer, and we honour the parents' dedication and determination, we weep for them. Anna and Michael were simply doing what they believed parents must do. It was no less heroic for that.

Anna was determined that Joe would recover, and she believed that by showing him, every day, her love for him and her family's commitment to him he would eventually return to them. She would stroke him, talk to him, perhaps even scold him gently to encourage him to wake. She and Michael talked to the doctors, too, who explained that little could be done and that Joe's present condition might continue for years or forever. When admitted to Concord, he was a young man, 22 years of age, with a powerfully beating heart. His ankles were slowly recovering, as was his thumb, though his ankles would never, in fact, be completely repaired, as the doctors explained, and it was unlikely that he would ever walk again.

On 3 June 1969, Michael received a telegram asking him to phone a senior nurse at Concord to give his permission for an urgent operation, the need for which must have become apparent overnight. This would have been the tracheotomy of which Joe would later speak with some awe and a little pride. His breathing must have become difficult for some reason, and the tracheotomy was an emergency procedure. Apart from that, there was little that could be done until Joe regained consciousness.

With some considerable lack of sensitivity, army headquarters continued to send progress reports by telegram to Michael as next of kin. For example: a telegram sent on 16 May, which read, in part, 'it is learned with regret that the condition of your son 2787617 private jarslow stawyskyj on 15 may 1969 was unchanged'. A handwritten note on one of the copies of the telegrams in Joe's official file states,

'E Comd [Eastern Command] advise that NOK [next of kin] are visiting regularly and do not require progress reports unless change of condition occurs'. And so the telegrams stopped. The next of kin could see for themselves. Every day.

Then a telegram came on 11 June 1969, advising Michael, 'with pleasure', that Joe 'had been removed from the very seriously ill list' and was 'progressing satisfactorily'. This was, apparently, the last telegram dispatched from army headquarters to Michael, and was sent because Joe had drifted into consciousness, if only briefly. For some time, according to the family, he was occasionally conscious; more often, however, he had relapsed back into a coma. But the army had him off their endangered list, and, from 26 September 1970, he was a matter for the Repat — the repatriation department. The army had more pressing matters in Vietnam.

The family watch changed somewhat after this, in the expectation that Joe would return to them permanently. The talk continued, and the care, but there now seemed to be some point to it all. Perhaps Joe would return to them, in full consciousness, at some point down the line, and they would have their son and brother back. Perhaps.

As time went on, Joe's condition did improve. There were longer periods of consciousness. He even made attempts to speak, but it was hard, if not impossible, to understand what he was trying to say. Yet his eyes could follow a visitor in the screened-off area, and he could be given a drink — water or some juice. Still, he remained at Concord without any hope of returning permanently to his home in Fairfield. Though, on five occasions in early 1970, he was given 'therapeutic leave' from Concord and stayed overnight at home. There was very great pleasure in having Joe home again, but it was apparent that Joe remained very damaged.

The army arranged to have Joe discharged from its service on the grounds that he was 'medically unfit'. Joe left the army on 27

September 1970, well exceeding his required two years period of service, because he had joined up, under compulsion, on 12 July 1967. An officer arrived at Concord on 8 October 1970 to explain to Joe his Re-establishment Benefits, and to tell him that he had recently been discharged from the army. The officer reported, for the benefit of the file, that 'due to Brain damage due to injuries received in Vietnam, Mr Stawyskyj was unable to understand most things that were said to him and was extremely difficult to communicate with because of a speech defect. Due to the extent of Mr Stawyskyj's injuries, I was unable to interview him.' However, the officer left a booklet explaining Re-establishment Benefits and Entitlements with his doctor, 'who would give it to Mr Stawyskyj's father', so that was alright then. The officer stated that Joe was probably entitled to a Totally and Permanently Incapacitated Pension.

Joe remained at Concord throughout 1971, making some improvement. He was finally discharged from Concord into the care of his parents sometime in 1972. He had 40 years of life in front of him.

Prognosis

REGAINING FULL CONSCIOUSNESS was a mighty first step for Joe, but it became apparent, after a while and gradually, that Joe suffered from a long-term and significant neurological problem. As he had drifted in and out of consciousness in the first weeks of his return from his coma, there had been a growing confidence that things were going to be fine. Then it became clear that this was not the case.

Joe's memory of his life until the moment of his 'accident' was fine: he could give you an engaging account of his early life. And then there was nothing. The family realised with growing surprise that something was wrong and then came to terms with the shock of what the doctors had been telling them. Joe had lost the capacity to retain his short-term memory. That is, he lost from recall everything he experienced, almost as soon as he had experienced it.

He might read a book, but what was the point? He would not remember any of the story at any point within it. He watched a great deal of television once he returned home, but he could not tell you, in an ad break, what had happened so far. He would engage you in conversation, but would not remember any of it even minutes later. On greeting him, I would always ask, 'What have you been up to, Joe?' 'Bugger all' was the invariable reply, even though he was taken out a bit, to the club and such like, had family visitors, and might have had something to talk about. Nothing stuck in his mind.

This is as life-denying an illness as could be imagined. Our memory, our stories, our little successes, our frustrations, our recall are essentially what makes us human. Joe lost the ability to hold onto any of the things in his life, and never regained it.

Think about human conversation, specifically male conversation. Men meet over a drink to talk about what? Well, sport, of course. How do you think the Swans will go on the weekend? Have you ever seen a gutsier footballer than Jude Bolton? Can the Dons ever regroup and recover? How long should so-and-so go on? Is Ian Thorpe the best Australian swimmer ever? And what an argument that would provoke. Then blokes might move on to politics or work. Everyone with an opinion, everyone more than capable of arguing several positions at once. Some men, older men, possibly, are smart enough to share their worries or concerns with their mates, and come to realise how much friendship means to them in life. But, in all their conversations, men and women draw on their recent and older memories to explain themselves, to assert themselves in the lives of family and friends, to exist, fundamentally, as persons.

Joe could do none of this from the moment he emerged from his coma. He recognised the people around his bed and knew, I'm sure, how much he was loved and treasured. He remained good with people, always deeply thankful to anyone who helped him, and, just to show what a peculiar thing the brain is, he could remember people, their names, and where they fitted in. At a family party, I might introduce him to a friend. 'Joe, this is Ros, my good friend. We work together and have done for years, and she has a boy, Alexander, whom we look after from time to time.' 'G'day, Ros', Joe would say. 'Bad luck about having to work with Michael.' It might be months and months until Joe would see Ros again. 'Hi, Ros', he would say. 'How's your boy?'

And, to make thinking about the brain even more worrying, let me tell you another story. We were taking Joe somewhere, home to his father for a meal at Bell Crescent, probably, after Joe had been moved into the nursing home at Hammondville. Driving up from Canberra,

Michalina and I had been bopping along to an ABBA CD. With Joe in the passenger seat beside me, I started the car and, naturally, the CD roared back into life, as I had forgotten it was there. Joe knew the words of every track as each came around and sang along with each song. Yet ABBA formed in 1972, and came to prominence in Australia from about 1975, well after Joe had lost his short-term memory. Nevertheless, their songs had lodged somewhere in his brain. Some would say the songs aren't noted for the sophistication of their words. That isn't the point. Joe could hold onto those words when almost nothing else at all stuck, people excepted.

So this was the worst of Joe's situation. Without short-term memory, he couldn't have a life as we understand it. He had a body that was healthy, vigorous, and strong, although he was unable to walk, because his wounds had never properly healed and his feet were a mess. He seemed to enjoy life, and certainly showed a dogged determination to go on living. But he couldn't participate in that life, beyond the immediate. Continuously, throughout the day, he would call to his dad for coffee or a cigarette, entirely unaware that just five minutes earlier he had smoked a cigarette and drunk a cup of coffee. So you would say, perhaps with some exasperation in your voice, 'But, Joe, you've just had one', and he would retreat, to sing out again in about 15 minutes.

He remembered how to play chess, and, in the early days, friends of the family, usually men, would drop in for a game with him. Later, when he bought a computer, he played both chess and solitaire on it. I don't play chess, but I think Joe must have been quite good at it. Once, with Michael and Michalina out somewhere, I was at Bell Crescent alone with Joe. I was in the kitchen, looking after the cooking that Michalina had left in my care, and Joe was in the front room playing chess on the computer. Suddenly, he let out an enormous yell, and I rushed in to see what was the matter. He sat there grinning. 'I beat the bugger', he said in triumph. I looked at the screen, which admitted that the computer could find 'no useful moves'. I would boast of Joe's triumph when his father and sister came back home; Joe would have forgotten.

Joe had other problems, too. His ankles had been repaired, but his wounds had never truly recovered, and 'sores' had to be dressed daily. His feet were woefully misshapen, and he needed specially built boots and slippers. He couldn't stand without assistance, and though, for his circulation, it was important that he stand and take some steps each day, he was never actually going to walk unassisted again. There was a fixed walking frame in the front room at which he could exercise, say six steps in one direction, six steps back. It was a constant battle to get him to do these exercises a few times each day, but they had to be done. Apart from that, he was either in bed or in his wheelchair, which he could propel rather expertly around the house.

Anna and Michael brought Joe back from Concord sometime in 1972. Anna, I have been told, was determined that Joe would make a better recovery than had been achieved at the hospital. She was certain that, with enough encouragement, he would learn to walk again, and perhaps his mind could be developed, too. She devoted herself to him. She saw him out of bed in the morning (Repat had provided a type of hospital bed, with a pole at the head of the bed and a steel triangle on a chain that Joe could grab onto to help himself out of bed). She gave him his breakfast. At some point in the morning, she gave him his shower and dressed his wounds. She would make him walk each day with the fixed walking frame, even, at one stage, attaching him to the rotary clothes line to make the walking more ambitious. It didn't work.

The house had been slightly modified and extended to cater for Joe. He took over the living room, and the family moved to a new back room beyond the small kitchen and dining room. The new room was pleasant, a large room with television and stereo, and, through a sliding door, it opened onto a new back verandah or porch with table and chairs, where Michael delighted to sit and think and, if he had an audience, talk. Michael remained at work at Borg-Warner, but Anna had given up work earlier to care for John and now Joe. Michalina graduated from the University of New South Wales in 1970, took a diploma of education in 1971, and began as a 'bonded teacher' in the New South Wales Education Department in 1972. Her first school was at Ingleburn, a south-western Sydney suburb and a tough assignment for a young teacher. She continued, of course, to live at home. John was still in primary school, a good boy, as was expected, trying to live a normal life.

Joe was home — this was all that mattered to Anna. With continuing payment from the army's not generous superannuation scheme (though it was not called that then) and a Totally and Permanently Incapacitated Pension, Joe was comfortable, though his parents were reluctant to touch any of his money, which he might need 'for later'. They might at least have charged him board. So life stretched out in front of Joe and Anna and Michael. Anna, at least, retained hope that Joe was on a path to improvement and that was her lode star. The medical people, however, offered no such encouragement.

For Repat, Joe was a file number in receipt of a pension. Special requests, such as for new boots, or a better bed, or a new wheelchair, would be assessed and usually granted. If Joe needed medical attention, he went to Concord, though there was little that could be done for him. If he needed respite, or Anna and Michael did, he would go to Lady Davidson hospital in Turramurra, and he did so perhaps once a year for a 'holiday'. Apart from that, he followed the same routine at Bell Crescent day in, day out, month in, month out.

And that was that. An awful casualty of the war in Vietnam, Australia's most unpopular war ever. One of its worst casualties, almost entirely forgotten by the Australian community. The community would pay the bills, small though they were. But the family would carry the burden.

Getting on with It

PEOPLE WERE KIND, of course they were. On 8 April 1969 (less than a fortnight since Joe's family had received their first news of his 'accident'), the chief manager of New South Wales for the ANZ Bank, Joe's former employer, wrote, 'I was very sorry to learn that your son was seriously wounded in action in Vietnam ... our sympathy goes to you in this worrying time'. He wrote again in early June: 'we have kept in contact with the Army since your son was wounded and we are extremely sorry to learn that he has not yet recovered from his injuries. We are relieved to know that he is now back in Australia where he can receive the best medical attention available ... if we, in the Bank, can be of any assistance to you, please don't hesitate to contact us.'

Joe received a nice, chatty letter from a friend whom he'd been in contact with, a Sister of Charity at St Mary's Convent, Liverpool, New South Wales. She was a friend of Joe's from school days, and the sister of one of Joe's good friends, Rod, who was also a conscript, but had not been sent overseas. Sister Mary Louisa wrote on 9 April 1969, 'I hope when this reaches you that you will be well enough to read it.' She had visited her mother at home the day before, and had learned that Joe was seriously ill: 'you don't know how sorry we all are. We had all hoped and prayed you would get out of it safely, but now the only thing to do is for you to get better as quickly as you can and be transferred home.' Joe had written to her from Vietnam, and she noted that 'it was terrific to receive [your letter]'. She told him that Parramatta lost to Manly last week in the rugby league, that a mutual friend had had a baby, and that she loved the children (48 infants) she was teaching. 'Some of the things they say and do are really delightful and I really am hard put not to laugh but I try to keep a straight face.' She promised to remember Joe and his parents in all her prayers: 'I only wish we could all do more.'

People expected that Joe would get better, and this is a natural assumption. Time heals everything, and medical advances, even in 1969, were so respected that it would be certainly unusual to envisage Joe as a chronic invalid for life. So the letters are hopeful and optimistic, expecting that Joe will resume his life at some point in the future. They are all the harder to read for that, now.

Joe was young — that was the whole point of conscription. In March 1969, he had just turned 22. Had Joe returned from Vietnam whole and hearty, he would have picked up with those old friends whom army life hadn't estranged, he would have kept many of his army mates, and he would have made new friends in the workplace. Vietnam would have remained important in his life, but life always moves on.

There's no second letter from Sister Mary Louisa among Joe's papers. It might have been written and then been lost, but I doubt it. The file is so complete. The young nun had written a friendly letter in the expectation that Joe would be showing good signs of improvement. That perhaps he would reply with a friendly letter of his own. It was hard to accept Joe's real condition and circumstances, that he would be a wheelchair-bound invalid for the rest of his life, that conversation with him could only focus on the immediate, and that you had to strain so hard to understand even a little of what he was trying to say. That he would never be able to write a sentence, let alone a letter; that the most he might do thereafter would be to sign his own name.

When Joe finally returned home permanently, to the care of his parents, some of his mates did make the effort to visit. Anna was extremely welcoming, and lavished food and drink on the boy or girl visiting. That was simply her way, but, in these circumstances, it was even more important. Yet, for the visitor, every visit was hard and, frankly, seemingly unrewarding. Joe really was 'buggered up', as his mates put it, and so there was little to talk about. Had Manly beaten Parramatta, as Sister Mary Louisa had claimed? Joe wouldn't know, would not know even the barest details of the footy. Could the boy or girl talk about dances and parties, gone or coming up? This would seem a bit heartless with Joe the way he was. Talk about work, who was marrying whom, who was having babies, who was buying a house, who was travelling? All that seemed heartless, too. What else was there to talk about? What could you do with this bloke?

So visits from mates dropped off pretty soon, and Joe lapsed further into a cocoon of family and routine. The family resented this, were hurt by it, for they knew Joe needed the contact, enjoyed it, that it enriched him. And yet, within a few months of his return home, Joe was as isolated as if he had remained at Concord forever. Michael and Anna were disappointed for Joe. He'd always had mates around; he'd always been generous and well liked. Perhaps, in some part of their understanding of Joe, Anna and Michael realised how hard it was for visitors to spend time with Joe. But they loved their boy, and they wanted others to love him, too.

On 7 July 1972, Ken Bromley, announcing himself as the secretary of the Wounded Servicemen's Convalescent Scheme — a major project, as he explained, of the Rotary Club of Surfers Paradise — wrote: 'Over the past six years, it has been my pleasure to look after nearly twelve hundred wounded men from all three services ... When it is convenient to you, Joe, we want to give you a fortnight's expense free convalescence under our scheme. I will arrange a first class return air passage from Sydney to Coolangatta for you and if you are married, your wife also. We take care of all accommodation, meals, tours, trips, cruises and other entertainment you may wish. Please let me know when you would like to join us.' He told Joe of the warm, sunny days of a Gold Coast winter, but warned that the nights could be a little cold.

The generosity of this offer is impressive. How much money must the Rotary Club of Surfers Paradise have raised to fund such magnificent support of wounded servicemen across six years? The club sought and gained assistance from the owners of accommodation such as motels, and from businesses such as restaurants and tour companies, and also from private donors. Even so, Rotary had raised a lot of money and given a lot of time, and continued to do so. Nearly 1,200 first-class airfares, accommodation, and hospitality in six years. What kindness there is in the world, what simple goodness.

It seems that Joe did not reply to this first letter — perhaps it all seemed just too hard — and so there was a second letter from Ken Bromley, perhaps more insistent. Among Joe's papers, there's a carbon copy of the reply sent to Bromley's second letter. Who wrote and typed it, I can't say. Joe says in his letter that he was 'overjoyed to receive your generous invitation', but even 'a few days away' would raise problems. 'Dear Ken', his letter explains, 'I am confined to a wheelchair and cannot walk, have a bath or use the amenities without someone to help me to stand up, and I am only able to walk when supported by another person. I am trying to walk on crutches but I am finding it hard to keep my balance. I am even dictating this letter'.

The letter is realistic. 'Unless you have at your convalescent home some nurse or person to look after persons like myself, such a prospect, however I would like to enjoy it, remains a dream for me for an indefinite time.' Although, he says, he would much like to spend some time 'with my wounded fellow servicemen'. He writes that he has a close friend, a wounded Second World War veteran, Jack Glass, who spent some time with him in hospital: 'I also have a speech impediment at present and Jack can communicate with me, as he is used to me now.' Perhaps he could come along, too, Joe writes, though he carefully explains that

Jack could not stand in for a nurse. 'If you can find a solution to my problem please reply and I will be on the plane quick smart.'

Miraculously, Joe did make the trip, in September 1972, though without his mate Jack Glass. There's an account of his visit in the *Surfers Paradise Mirror*, 20–26 September 1972. Joe is described as 'the most seriously wounded of the 1200 servicemen to visit Surfers Paradise' so far under the scheme. He took his first steps, unaided, at a Rotary dinner at the Iluka Motel, the newspaper reported, and 'his feat was wildly cheered by other wounded soldiers currently convalescing under the scheme'. It's nice to think that this might have been a turning point for Joe, that he was on the way to walking, that he might, one day, walk without support and assistance. But it was a pipe dream, a newspaper romance and fiction. It was part of a belief system that postulates that all wounded soldiers, all seriously ill young people, must get better.

Joe needed constant care, and could do very little indeed for himself. Even the *Surfers Paradise Mirror* recognised this. Joe was accompanied on his trip, the newspaper said, 'by Corporal Michael Taylor of the Royal Australian Army Medical Corps who was assigned by the Army to assist him'. You can see, surely, the hand of Ken Bromley in that neat arrangement. Joe had a dream, Bromley explained, to walk unaided up the aircraft steps at the end of his convalescence on the Coast. I can hear Joe saying that. Many years later, he told me that he would like to drive a car again. He was a dreamer. And if he could live with some hope that one day he would be getting on with it, well then, so much the better for him. Despite everything, Joe never seemed to let his circumstances get him down. 'I will walk again', he seemed to think; 'I will recover', he seemed to dream.

Joe didn't walk up the steps of the aircraft when it was time to go back home to Sydney. Perhaps even those few steps at the Rotary dinner were more in the eyes of the beholders or some special effect of Joe's iron determination and showmanship.

The trip must have been exciting and eventful in a routine life. It was his last such trip for many years. The walls of his home in Bell Crescent closed in on him. His mother fed, clothed, and bathed him; his father brought him out onto the back porch when he was working in the nearby veggie patch, for companionship. His sister and his brother did what they could for him. His aunty and uncle talked and chaffed with him, as did his three cousins. All around him, he saw people working, people growing up, people getting good jobs and making good friends. If he ever resented his awful plight, he never said so. 'Oh', Michael would say. 'Joe's Joe.'

Anzac Day

FIFTH BATTALION, ROYAL AUSTRALIAN REGIMENT, returned to Australia from its second tour in Vietnam in February 1970. Twenty-five of its soldiers on this second tour had been killed in action and 202 had been wounded in action. When they returned to Australia, permanent members of the army went on leave before resuming their lives of service. Bill Grassick retired from the army in 1991, having reached the rank of colonel; Brian Burton became a warrant-officer class-one, and was, for a time, regimental sergeant-major of the combined 5/7 Battalion, Royal Australian Regiment.

National servicemen left the army as soon as their two years were served, most of them leaving soon after coming home. 'There was no difference at all between the national servicemen and the regulars while they were with the battalion', Bill Grassick observed, but every one of them would go their separate ways now. Many of those who had served in Vietnam came together each Anzac Day to remember their mates who had been killed and to catch up with each other, delighted to discover where each one's life journey was taking him.

Siggy Jablonski, his duty done, returned to his job at the Commonwealth Bank, resuming the life the army had interrupted. He had known Joe in 5RAR, but they had not been close mates. Both were in A Company, but Siggy had been in 3 Platoon while Joe was in 2 Platoon. On the day of the mine, Siggy had boarded the truck that Joe was on, but was ordered off it, and he jumped onto the truck third in line. In war, there is good luck and bad luck. Safely back in civilian life, Siggy married a German visitor he had met in Sydney, Ute. In expectation of many trips to Germany, Siggy left the bank and joined Qantas, where he had a long and very successful career. He and Ute had one daughter, Nicky.

Siggy's mother died in 1977, and, at the wake after the funeral, Siggy got talking to an older man, a Polish family friend named Stan. Stan began asking Siggy about his experience in Vietnam, and Siggy thought this was a bit unusual, as, from his perspective, it had all been quite a long time ago. Siggy asked Stan why he was interested. 'There is a friend of mine,' he said, 'a Ukrainian/Russian woman, Lala, who lives across the road from Ukrainian people, and they have a son who was badly wounded in Vietnam. I play chess with him from time to time, and he talks about his war a bit. I just wanted to know more.' Siggy asked Stan for the veteran's name and was astonished to be told that the veteran was called Joe Stawyskyj. 'What, is he alive?' Siggy asked incredulously. 'We all thought he had died.'

Anzac Day was approaching, and Siggy decided to ask Joe if he would like to go to the march in Sydney with him. Everyone would be amazed and delighted to see Joe, as no one had ever heard a thing about him, really, since he had been taken to hospital by the American helicopter. So Siggy rang Joe to invite him to the march, and the reunion that would follow it, but was pretty swiftly rebuffed. He can't remember if Joe explained why he wouldn't march with his mates, but he does remember that Joe was quite strong in saying no.

Siggy wasn't discouraged, and met up with Joe at home a few times. They got on well and were fast on the road to becoming good mates. The next year, 1978, Joe made contact with Siggy and asked if he could go to the Anzac Day march and the reunion. Siggy was delighted, and arranged a taxi for both of them.

In 1978, there were still First World War veterans in the march, and many Second World War veterans. As the older men aged and deteriorated physically, they were placed in army vehicles and even in taxis at the front of the entire march immediately after the march leader. The numbers of vehicles increased each year. Siggy didn't want Joe isolated in that way, separate from his mates, in a taxi with a couple of other veterans whom he would not have known anyway. If Joe was to march, Siggy wanted him with his 5RAR mates, in the thick of things, where he belonged. So, on this first march, he hid Joe at the back of the battalion, hoping that the officials wouldn't notice. He would push the wheelchair himself, for the entire route of the march, so that there would be no fuss. Joe was happy to go along with all of this.

So there he was, back with his mates, remembering their names, laughing and joking, proudly wearing his medals, taking an appropriate and proper part in Australia's most sacred ceremony, the annual remembrance of all those who have died in wars in the service of their country. Joe was sharing the march with men who had fought at Lone Pine and Quinn's Post, at Pozieres and Mont St Quentin, on the Kokoda Track, and at El Alamein, in the skies over Europe and the Pacific, or in ships on all the oceans of the world. Marching with men who had been at Nui Dat, too, who had fought in the battle of Binh Ba or in Operation Camden or on dozens of patrols. No one ever thought to tell Siggy that Joe shouldn't be where he was, and, as each year passed, his place at the back of the battalion was not only accepted, but also expected.

Until, that is, the officers thought differently. Colin Khan had stayed on in the army after returning from Vietnam. He had left the Defence Force in 1986 with the rank of brigadier, and then served for ten years with the Australian Federal Police. As he'd been the battalion's commanding officer during its second tour in Vietnam, he would lead the 5RAR component of the Sydney Anzac Day march whenever his duties allowed. He was popular with the men, and they were always pleased when he could be with them. One year, no one can precisely remember when, but it was not too long after Joe had begun to march with his mates, 'Genghis' gave Siggy an order: 'When I'm in town, I want Joe next to me', he said. 'He's our mascot.'

When Khan couldn't march, the officer leading 5RAR would follow his example. Joe would always be at the front, next to the commanding officer, right behind the banner, cheered as 5RAR was cheered each year when the battalion first stepped into public view. Soon, the ABC TV commentary team started to notice the bloke in the wheelchair at the head of 5RAR, and would make mention of him, even going to the trouble of learning his name. People in the crowd would sing out to him once they had got his name, and Joe played up to all of this. He enjoyed the attention. He had a smile and a wave for anyone who called out to him — and for everyone else, for that matter.

For 34 years, Siggy pushed Joe and his wheelchair for the entire length of the march. Then he took Joe to the reunion and watched out for him, a bit. Siggy and Joe became great mates. Joe got to know Ute, and delighted to watch Nicky growing up, as there was a special bond between them. It was almost as if Joe had found a second family, one that was always very welcome at Bell Crescent.

At the reunion after the march, with his mates, Joe would let his hair down. Jim Beam and Coke was his drink, 'no ice', and he was never short of blokes offering to buy him a refresher. It was hard to get a bloke in a wheelchair into clubs and pubs in the early days, with stairs and doors to be negotiated and tables to be moved to get Joe about, but nothing was ever too much trouble. One year, 5RAR held their reunion down at Camden, about 65 kilometres south-west of Sydney, and still they took Joe with them and still he had a great time. That year, Siggy remembers, there was dancing, and Joe was on the dance floor, in his wheelchair, creating havoc and laughing his head off. Neither Michael nor Anna worried about what time Joe got home on Anzac Day, and they turned a blind eye to evidence that Joe might have enjoyed himself a little too much. 'Something Joe ate upset him', Siggy would tell Anna.

'To us, Joe was still 20', Bill Grassick said of Joe's annual appearance at Anzac Day. 'He could remember things that we had long forgotten, and we were amazed by his cheerfulness and his determination. He was the worst wounded of anyone in the battalion, and yet he turned up year after year to be with his mates and to honour all those who had died serving their country.' For the men of 5RAR, Joe Stawyskyj ('Freddie' to most of them) was a man to honour, to admire, and to celebrate.

A Second Tragedy

ONE DAY, OUT OF THE BLUE, Joe said something that we had never heard before and would never hear again. It stunned us. Michalina and I were with Joe; Michael was elsewhere. 'I think I killed my mother', he said. We were so shocked that we sat in silence. Then Michalina's natural resilience kicked in: 'Don't be silly, Joe, be quiet, don't say such silly things.' The moment passed.

Making Joe better had been the sole focus of Anna's life from the moment that she learned that Joe was 'very seriously ill'. She watched over him throughout the long months of his coma, stroked him, encouraged him to wake, gave him almost all of her attention. When he came home, she did everything for him: cooked, washed, bathed, dressed, fed, and nurtured him. She could be hard on him with tough love, not allowing him to slacken in his efforts to walk again and return to something like full health. But she had become, overnight, in her sister-in-law's words, 'an old lady'. Yet she was not one. When Joe was blown up, Anna was 43 years of age.

Anna was very well liked by those who knew her. She was generous, fun-loving, kind, and positive. She and Michael had a special bond forged in their shared experiences as slaves of the Nazis. This understanding had taken them from war-torn Europe to Australia and 20 years of good, quiet, and happy family life.

A friend, who is a little older than I am, asked me to look at other Australian marriages affected by war. His father had joined the air force in 1940 and had left Australia for Canada in 1941, as a member of the Empire Air Training Scheme. He served in the European theatre in RAF Coastal Command once his training was completed, and only returned to Australia in February 1945, after almost four years overseas. He had left behind a wife and one son (my friend). The wife had not worked in the paid workforce during the war years, had lived in the house her husband had provided on marriage, and had raised her son. The money that her husband allotted to her from his pay was adequate for her needs, and she lived an independent life.

My friend explained that there were tensions of readjustment in the marriage after his father returned from the war. Perhaps the airman felt that his wife never tried to understand the constant fear with which he lived while he was on duty in the air; perhaps he thought that she did not appreciate the restrictions and limitations with which he lived during the war. Perhaps she felt that he didn't understand the loneliness with which she lived and the struggle for existence as a single mother in wartime Australia. There was a great possibility for misunderstanding and resentment in this marriage. Both husband and wife had been living, in their own ways, as individuals, and they possibly chafed at the restrictions imposed on their freedom once married life was resumed. For whatever reasons, the marriage was not particularly happy for long periods thereafter, though it might have seemed so to observers.

A similar picture of an Australian post-war marriage is given by historian John Rickard in his moving book *An Imperial Affair: portrait of an Australian marriage*. Rickard's father also served overseas for a long period, in England, with the Royal Australian Air Force, and also left a wife and son at home in Australia. After a similarly tense period of adjustment to post-war realities, Rickard's mother discovered that her husband had entered into a passionate and quite long-lasting affair with a married English woman during his time of service overseas. She was horrified and angry and, taking her children, separated from her husband briefly until induced back into the marriage. Thereafter, the marriage staggered along, with many moments of recrimination and difficulty.

In both cases, there was a gulf of understanding between the wives' lives in Australia and the husbands' lives overseas. This is not to lay blame in any direction, but to state merely that such disruption over such long periods must have complicated these relationships. By way of contrast, Michael and Anna shared an understanding of the horrors, dangers, and drudgery of wartime Germany from the position of the lowest of the low. They knew exactly how each had lived, what pressures they were subjected to, and which survival techniques each had adopted. That they had survived was a triumph in itself, but it was also important that they understood each others' lives and sufferings, and the sadness in leaving their much loved home families. They clung to each other in a new and strange land, giving even greater strength and comfort in their marriage.

No one should look into another marriage with a view to understanding it, as each marriage is unique to those involved. If we can find comfort and peace, success in mutual hopes, and victory in mutual fears, if we have given something to our families and our communities, then I think we may say that we have 'done alright'. In 1967, before Joe received his letter from the Department of Labour and National Service, I think Anna and Michael were well entitled to feel satisfied with what they had achieved. As Michael often said, 'so far, so good'. The family was modestly comfortable, thanks to great hard work from both of them, and the three children seemed happy and were making good progress, each in their own way. Michael's brother had joined him from Poland, and now his family, too, was well housed, well off, and making good progress. Anna and Michael had good friends, were well liked in the Ukrainian community, and gave back to that community insofar as they could.

Joe's tragedy blew this life apart. Not only did Joe's friends drop out of the scene, but also, to a large degree, so did Anna and Michael's. Anna had little time for anything or anyone but Joe. She believed that he had to be the focus of all her effort and endeavour. Even her other children might have suffered in her single-minded care of Joe, might have been left more to their own devices than Anna may have wanted.

Michael once said to me that people had told him and Anna that perhaps it might be better if Joe went into care, where he might receive more-appropriate and more-skilled assistance. If he went into a home, people said, the burden of his care would be taken over by several carers, including nurses, physios, cooks, and cleaners. Michael and Anna, these kind friends said, would, of course, continue to be involved with Joe in his new home, but they would have some time and space for themselves. Michael looked at me, as he told me this, in frank amazement and disbelief that people could be so blind, so callous. 'We were his parents,' he said, 'he was our son.' And that was the end of the matter.

But Anna was worn out in the service of her son. There was the physical toil of dealing with his increasingly heavy body, though he was never a big man. There was the constancy of his demands and needs. The cry for a cigarette or a cup of coffee, the need for three good meals a day; the bathing of him each day and the dressing of his wounds, the supervision of what exercise he could be encouraged to take, the chore of keeping him active and interested in life. It was all-consuming, relentless, unstoppable.

There was also the psychological toll of Joe's circumstances, which was equally as demanding and as constant. Anna never ceased to believe that Joe could be made better, whereas others began to see a deterioration rather than an improvement. She never ceased to grieve, daily, for the situation her son was in. He might have had a good job with promotion and respect. He might have had a wife, she thought, to love and nurture him as his mother had always done. There might have been children, she imagined, to whom Joe would have been a wonderful father, and who would have delighted her later years, and whom she could smother in love. Gina said that Anna was never very far away from tears throughout the remainder of her life after Joe's tragedy. She lived with a permanent sadness and grief, which she had to hide from Joe as best she could.

Is it any wonder that her once-strong peasant's heart simply gave out when Anna was 60? Without warning, Anna collapsed. She was taken to hospital immediately, but died within a few days. The shock of the loss, the suddenness of the death, dominated the funeral a few days later. That this strong, resilient, determined woman had gone was almost beyond the family's comprehension. Friends poured out their love to Michael, to Michalina, and to John, and they grieved for a family now in terrible circumstances. Without the time for any preparation at all, Anna had gone. Leaving behind a distraught husband, grieving children, and Joe, who would come to think that she had died out of her love and determination for him. Which she had.

Michael Takes Over

ANNA DIED IN APRIL 1987, just a month short of her 61st birthday. Michael would turn 65 on 3 June 1987, and had been contemplating compulsory retirement on that date for some time. He was already looking forward to more leisure, though you could be certain that much of his leisure time would be spent in work. He would renew his commitment to the vegetable garden and the garden in general. There were always jobs around the house and little jobs for neighbours in the street. Perhaps he and Anna and Joe might spend more time at the little holiday home they had built at Gwandalan on Lake Macquarie. They all liked it up there. But, even at Gwandalan, the lawns needed mowing and there were repairs and improvements to make to the house. There would also be more time for cards with Gina and John in the evening at Bell Crescent, and more time for sitting and thinking.

Michael left work immediately after Anna died. He had to. Who else could look after Joe? Dreams of the pleasant, restful retirement evaporated instantly as Michael now threw himself into the routine that had been Anna's since 1972. He would cook for Joe, which meant, in fact, that he would have to learn how to cook — and quickly. He would care for Joe as Anna had done in every detail of Joe's life.

Mercifully, though, he would not have to bathe Joe or dress his wounds. Someone had let the family know of the existence of the district nursing service run by the local council, which could give Joe the daily attention he needed. When I arrived on the scene as Michalina's new friend in 1989, the nurse was a lively, engaging woman called Jenny. She was younger than any of us, highly efficient, bubbling with good fun, and earnest as Joe's nurse. Her arrival at Bell Crescent, usually in the early afternoon, was a real occasion and a source of pleasure and delight. Joe teased her, as he always did with visitors, and Jenny gave back as good as she got.

Michael had worked as a machinist at Borg-Warner for nearly 25 years, but not quite. Even so, in the circumstances, he was made a member of the 25 Year Club, given his gold watch, of which he was very proud, and extended an invitation to the club's annual dinner. He received just over $9,000 from Borg-Warner's superannuation plan, and would live on the Australian old-age pension for the remainder of his days. So money would be tight, but debt-free; he would manage. Michael would only touch Joe's money to pay for his son's medicines and (when these could be arranged) holidays.

Sending Michael his entitlements, the manager of employee relations at Borg-Warner sent him the company's thanks and best wishes: 'May I take this opportunity to thank you sincerely for your many years of loyal service with the Company. The knowledge and experience you gained over almost a quarter of a century with the Company will be greatly missed. However we understand and sympathise with your reasons for taking early retirement and we trust that your future years will be blessed with good health and contentment'. Nice thoughts, of course, but Michael realised that he was facing a challenging future.

People rallied to help. Gina and John called in every day to lend a hand and to give Michael some companionship. Michael's younger son, John, still lived at home, as any unmarried Ukrainian boy would be expected to do. He had graduated brilliantly in arts/law from the University of Sydney and had his foot on the bottom rungs of a ladder that would take him to the heights of commercial law in Australia.

Michalina had moved to Melbourne to work as a teacher, was single, and was sharing accommodation with a friend. There was an expectation from some that Michalina should return home to take over her mother's role in the family, but Michalina resisted this. Instead, she found a senior position in education at the Australian War Memorial and moved to a home of her own in Canberra. This meant that she was much closer to Fairfield, but not actually living at home, and she began her fortnightly, often weekly, journeys to Sydney to shop, to cook, and to care for her father and disabled brother. She made no fuss about this, and only close friends would have known of her commitment and loyalty to her family.

Michael was good with Joe; they rubbed along together. Settling quickly into a routine, there was always something to be done. Joe would spend much of his day in the front room watching television, or playing chess or cards on his computer. Michael had a television set in the back room, where he could relax when all the chores were done. The council provided home help a couple of times a week, and both Michael and Joe struck up a real friendship with the middle-aged Irish woman, Marie, who did so much work around the home for them. Michael liked to watch sport, particularly rugby league and cricket, but he picked up Aussie Rules very quickly under my tutelage and we enjoyed watching games together.

The remarkable thing about this quiet, enclosed life in a quiet, enclosed street where little had changed across the years, was how content both Michael and Joe appeared to be. Michael would never lose his sadness about 'when this thing happened to Joe', as he always expressed it, but he made the best of his lot. A few years later, there was the possibility of a new partner, but — when she made it a condition of a shared life that Joe be put in a home, saying she could not take on the burden of his care — the prospect was terminated immediately. It was as if Michael had made a personal vow to Anna that Joe would live at home and be cared for there, a vow that he would never break. Perhaps it was not so much a vow as a shared and agreed understanding.

Joe lived his life in seeming contentment; at least, he never complained and simply took each day as it came. He didn't ever seem bored or dispirited by his situation, and was always cheerful and welcoming when anyone visited.

In October 1994, John married into a respected northern Tasmanian family, and we all travelled to Tassie for the wedding, including Joe. Michalina was on hand to ensure that Joe behaved himself, and he did, and, despite wild weather as the night went on, it was a rollicking good party. When John's first child and therefore Michael's first grandchild, Zoe, was born in 1996, Michael became 'gee-dough' (Ukrainian for grandpa) — eventually to four granddaughters. His love for them was so obvious, but in a shy sort of way. After John, Susie, and Zoe had left from an early visit, when Zoe was about three months old, I said to Michael what a fine little baby she seemed to be: 'so far, so good' was his super-cautious reply.

Around the time of Zoe's birth, Michael began a refrain that would become more insistent as the years passed: 'my head doesn't work', he would say. What do you mean by that, exactly, I would reply, somewhat amused by the complaint. 'I go to the shops to buy these things,' he would say, 'and, when I get home, I discover I've forgotten one or two of the things I had set off to buy, and I get so cross.' In truth, we took little notice of this at first, and I told him not to worry, as it was simply a consequence of getting old. Gradually, however, it became apparent that there was a real problem and that Michael was in the early stages of the dreaded and cursed Alzheimer's disease.

We asked Marie to increase the days she worked for Michael and Joe, as a temporary solution, but it became clear, eventually, that Joe was too big a burden to keep at home. In 2003, Joe was transferred to Poate House, a high-care nursing home within the HammondCare facilities at Hammondville, 15 kilometres from Bell Crescent. It was a huge change for Joe, which he took pretty well, although he complained at first that he was unhappy living among 'the dead and the dying', as he put it. But he accepted the change, and soon became a much loved part of the place. Within a relatively short time, he also became the longest-surviving resident at Poate House, and would retain that title until his own death, nearly ten years later.

Now Michael was on his own. After a relatively minor traffic accident on the way back from the shops, the police explained to John that it was probably best if Michael stopped driving. He was already a homebody, and this reduced his time away from home even further. Michael came to Canberra for short breaks, but, even in the car on the way down, he would begin complaining that he wanted to go home. Home for him now was everything, although he was happy to go to the club for a couple of hours to play the poker machines. He held out constant hopes of a good win, yet he strongly believed that the machines were cheating him.

Michael's mind retired gradually but inexorably. He rarely left the back room, and even began sleeping there. This man of words, this marvellous storyteller, retreated into himself, and conversation became difficult — in the end, impossible.

At long last, Michalina and John made the decision that Michael would have to go to the dementia unit at Hammondville. Michael did what was asked of him. It was an immensely sad occasion when I drove him away from Bell Crescent for the last time. He had a nice room in his new home and pleasant common rooms, but Michael was bewildered and uncomfortable.

Transferred to Poate House for his last days, Michael slipped out of life on 12 February 2007, a shrunken little old man so very much loved. Joe, whose certainty of an afterlife never wavered, said that it was good that his mother and father were together again.

Poate House

'HOW'S POP?' JOE ASKED not infrequently in the months after Michael's death. It was a ghastly question, reminding us of both our loss and the awfulness of Joe's circumstances. Gradually, however, Joe began to retain the information that his father had died, and seemed to accept this. Although we visited regularly, we didn't know much about Joe's life at Poate House, because he couldn't tell us much. 'What have you been doing, Joe?' I asked at the start of each visit. 'Bugger all', he would reply, the same as ever. In fact, at a case-management meeting, one of the staff reported that he had activities almost every day of the week, and some excursions. We were told that Joe threw himself into the life at Poate with enthusiasm and generosity.

We took him away from Poate most visits to a local club for a drink, lunch, and the pokies. It wasn't much, but it was at least a change of scenery. Michalina was adept at getting Joe into the car (as Michael had been, too): wheelchair right up to the front passenger door; help Joe to stand, with him holding onto the door; slip the wheelchair away and help him swing around until he could manoeuvre himself to be aligned with the seat; watch carefully as he lowered himself onto the seat; then crouch down to help him lift his legs and feet into the car. Getting him out of the car was a little harder, but also only a matter of a few minutes.

Poate House didn't permit residents to smoke indoors, naturally, so we usually sat out in the gardens with Joe. Sometimes, another smoker would join us, one with whom Joe would be on good terms. But we came to realise that this friendship could last only a few months at most, as no resident, apart from Joe, was going to last long in this facility for the very sick. Most residents were considerably older than Joe, too. And though a doctor once remarked that Joe's body was in fact that of a man 20 years older than Joe's chronological age (such had been the damage to it), he was very much better off than most of the other residents. Nevertheless, the landmine so many years ago was still wreaking its havoc.

Anzac Day remained a highlight of the year for Joe. Michalina would ensure that his jacket was freshly laundered, that his medals were in good repair and easily available to the staff, and that Joe had sufficient Cabcharge vouchers and enough money for his day out. The staff at Poate were discreet about the time of Joe's return home after Anzac Day, and his condition on arrival. He was never able to tell us how the day had gone, but we imagined he had a pretty good time.

Walking back to the car after a visit in October 2012, Michalina remarked that she thought Joe had been in especially good form. He seemed more lively and more interested in things than we had seen for some time, she said. I agreed: it had been wonderful to find him in such good fettle. 'We might think of sending him on a holiday', Michalina said, 'if we could iron out the problem of a carer.' I agreed with that, too, and we began to wonder how we might arrange this, and where Joe might go. There had been a place in Queensland that catered for wheelchair-bound people, and Joe had been there a couple of times, but, sadly, it had closed. We would try to find something similar, we agreed. He deserved a bit of a break from Poate.

It was a Friday afternoon a couple of weeks later. Michalina had returned from an overseas work trip, and I had picked her up at the airport. We wanted to pick up something she had bought at a shop before she left Australia, and she was walking towards the shop when her phone rang. It was the sister in charge at Poate House. They were a bit worried about Joe, who seemed off-colour and listless, so they had sent him around to Liverpool Hospital for observation and a check-up. Speaking to a doctor at the hospital a couple of hours later, Michalina learned that they thought Joe had suffered a heart attack. 'No need to come up now', the doctor said. 'Tomorrow will be fine.' But at 1.30 a.m., the hospital rang. 'You should come straightaway', someone said, 'if you wish to see your brother alive' — and we were on the road shortly afterwards.

They are depressing places, hospitals, at night, at a time of personal or family crisis. Footsteps ring out down long empty corridors; night lights give an eerie feel to the place. Joe was in intensive care, barely conscious, and obviously in a bad way. Later, in the morning, there was a meeting with the senior cardiologist, the intensive-care doctor, the senior intensive-care nurse, and a grief counsellor. 'You need to prepare yourselves for Joe's death', Michalina and John were told. 'He cannot survive the damage that has been already done, and it will be a matter of hours to the end.' You don't know Joe, I thought to myself, you don't know how he fights for life.

And he did, to the surprise of the medical staff. Within a week or so, he was returned to Poate, and the staff there were very glad to have him back. He was a bit of a celebrity. 'You gave us a fright, Joe, and was it quiet around here with you off on holidays.'

But Joe was now bedridden. He could be wheeled into a dayroom or the dining room for a bit of diversion, but he could no longer go outside for a cigarette or control his life as he had been doing for nearly ten years at Poate. He was diminished, he appeared startled by the change of circumstances, and, we felt, he was not very happy. These were sad days, but they didn't last long.

Within a couple of weeks, Joe was back at Liverpool Hospital. There were further heart attacks, perhaps a couple of strokes, they suspected, and no force could keep him going now. We said our goodbyes, told him how much we loved him, and watched in intense sadness as he slipped from life. It was sad to see the real sense of loss among the staff at Poate House when Michalina told people there that Joe had died. They had loved him, too.

Epilogue

JOE DIED ON 20 DECEMBER 2012. The funeral was held at the Ukrainian church of St Andrew at Lidcombe on 24 December, possibly the worst day of the year for a funeral. Although, since Ukrainian Christmas is celebrated on 7 January, the church and the priest were not too greatly inconvenienced.

Michalina and John had no idea how many people would attend the funeral. Not too many, they thought, given what day it was and how people are always extraordinarily rushed on that day. We, as the family, had entered the church before most of the congregation, and were sitting in the front rows, close to the coffin. I had been asked to read the Epistle. When I turned to face the congregation, having walked up towards the altar, I was astonished. There was a very large number of people present, quite a number of them Joe's mates from 5RAR — Siggy Jablonski, still working hard on Joe's behalf, had put the word out.

This was the church from which Anna and Michael had been farewelled, and Joe's Uncle John. It was hard for me, on that hot December afternoon, not to be thinking of Michael and the emotions that arose as we said goodbye to him. I listened to the ancient Ukrainian liturgy, which dated back to the church at Constantinople; these same words had been spoken from the altar for Michael's funeral, and for Anna's; the same words had been spoken in the village of Banyca for the funeral of Stefan Stawyskyj during the years of the Second World War. Stefan had served the Austro-Hungarian

Empire all those years ago as a conscripted soldier. His son Michael was unable to attend his funeral as he was a conscription slave worker in Germany. It was unthinkable. Conscription and war had radically altered the lives of these two men, father and son, Stefan and Michael.

It was extraordinary that conscription and war reached into the life of a third generation of the Stawyskyj family. Anna and Michael had travelled to the ends of the world, as they understood it, to free themselves and their children from the curse of European hatreds and jealousies. And yet Joe had been conscripted into the Australian army and had been sent to war. The third man in three generations (among the few men of the family) to accept what was asked of him, to do his duty, and to serve during war. His fate was far worse than that of either his father or his grandfather, and his sufferings had a far worse impact on his own parents and his sister and brother than the fate of either Stefan or Michael on their immediate families.

Michael's mother was never to see her son again after he was taken from Banyca, but at least she had the consolation of knowing that Michael had survived in Germany and had started a new life in Australia. He had found a fine wife to share his hardships and successes, he had built his own home, he had brought up, with Anna, three healthy, happy, and successful children. Though the old lady missed her son, she was happy for his new life. Anna and Michael took much consolation from the lives and successes of Michalina and John, but their grief for Joe was a constant in their lives. As the Ukrainian nuns sang and chanted, as the Ukrainian priest blessed the coffin and consoled the congregation as best he could, it was hard not to think of the way that war had twisted and tormented these good people.

Towards Anzac Day 2013, Michalina said how tough it would be for Siggy this year. For 34 years, every year, Siggy had pushed Joe's wheelchair and Joe along the entire length of the march, and had cared for him throughout the day. He received help, of course, and he was always warm in his thanks to those who came to Joe's aid, but Siggy was the main man, the main force.

Siggy sent us a photograph through the internet shortly after the march. The photographer is in front of the 5RAR banner, which is in the background. In the foreground, there is a wheelchair, unoccupied. On it is draped an Australian flag, on which sits an Australian Army slouch hat. Siggy pushed this wheelchair the length of the march, again, and all his mates supported him in remembrance of Joe. They, and many in the crowd, missed and mourned Joe. War had done terrible things to this family, across the 20th century and beyond. But people showed that they cared and understood the cruelty, the suffering that war causes across the generations.

Acknowledgements

I COULD NOT HAVE WRITTEN this book if I had not become a part, through marriage, of the Stawyskyj family. I thank Michael, Joe, and John for their genuine warmth in welcoming me into the family. I thank, most particularly, my wife, Michalina, for her love and generosity throughout a happy marriage.

I thank Michalina and John for their generous support of this project, and for the trust they have placed in me to tell their story.

I thank 'Aunty' Gina Stawiski and her son Stephen for their generous insights into her family's life in Australia.

I thank Joe's great mate, Siggy Jablonski, for the love and support he gave to Joe and his family over many years. I thank also Siggy's wife, Ute, who joined Siggy in this, and their daughter, Nicky, who had a special bond with Joe.

I thank my agent, Clare Forster of Curtis Brown, for her enthusiastic approach to the outlines of the idea and for finding me a publisher so quickly. I thank her, too, for her close reading of the text and for her suggestions for improvement.

I thank Henry Rosenbloom and Scribe for taking on this book and for their support of it in all the stages of its production. I particularly thank my editor at Scribe, David Golding, for his close reading of the text, his care in preventing me from falling into error, and his deeply sympathetic concern to make the book what we would all want it to be.

I thank my good friends and 'constant readers' Dr Stephen Foster and Paul Macpherson, who read drafts carefully and made numerous helpful suggestions. My good friend Bill Fogarty, ex-7RAR, read the sections relating to Vietnam and saved me from errors and mistakes.

Through Siggy Jablonski, I contacted former members of 5RAR, and I thank them for their co-operation and insights. I particularly thank Brian Burton, Bill Grassick, and Barry Greene.

I thank staff at the National Library of Australia and the Australian War Memorial for their assistance with research.

Finally, I thank, as I always do, our family — Katherine and Mark, Matilda and Nina; Jane and Toby, Ada and Eugene — for their love and support and their inspiration.